Personal Best

Workbook

A1
Beginner

Series Editor
Jim Scrivener

Author
Daniel Barber

1	My life	p3
2	People and things	p10
3	Food and drink	p16
4	Daily life	p22
5	All about me	p28
6	Places	p34
7	All in the past	p40
8	Travel	p46
9	Shopping	p52
10	Time out	p58
	WRITING PRACTICE	p64

Richmond

UNIT 1

My life

HELLO — LANGUAGE

GRAMMAR: The verb *be* (*I*, *you*)

1 Match 1–7 with a–g.

1 ____ you a student?   a Yes
2 Yes, I ____.   b not
3 No, I'm ____.   c I'm a
4 ____, you are.   d Are
5 No, you ____.   e 're not
6 ____ student.   f You're
7 ____ a teacher.   g am

2 ▶ 1.1 Complete the sentences. Listen and check.

> A Good morning. ¹_____ you a student?
> B Oh, hello. Yes, I ²_____.
> A Welcome to the school. My name's John. I'm a teacher here. And you ³_____ ... ?
> B ⁴_____ Veronica. Nice to meet you. ⁵_____ I in your class?
> A No, you ⁶_____. I'm ⁷_____ your teacher. ⁸_____ in Min's class.
> B OK, thank you.

VOCABULARY: Classroom language

3 Match sentences 1–6 with pictures a–f.

1 Excuse me, what does this word mean?   _f_
2 I'm sorry, I don't understand.   ____
3 How do you say "*arigatou*" in English? ____
4 Can you repeat that, please?   ____
5 How do you spell that?   ____
6 Sorry I'm late.   ____

4 Order the words to make sentences.

1 8 / to / books / page / open / your
   _____.

2 books / close / your
   _____.

3 turn / 7 / page / to
   _____.

4 at / look / picture / the
   _____.

5 and / listen / repeat
   _____.

6 in / pairs / work
   _____.

PRONUNCIATION: The alphabet

5 ▶ 1.2 Write the other letters of the alphabet. Listen and check.

1	/eɪ/	n**a**me	Aa, Hh, ____, ____
2	/iː/	s**ee**	Bb, Cc, ____, ____, ____, ____, ____, ____, ____
3	/ɛ/	b**e**d	Ff, ____, ____, ____, ____, ____
4	/ay/	**I**'m	____, ____
5	/ow/	n**o**	____
6	/uː/	y**ou**	Qq, ____, ____
7	/ɑ/	**a**re	

1A LANGUAGE

GRAMMAR: The verb *be* (*he, she, it*)

1 Choose the correct words to complete the sentences.

1. A *Are* / *Is* that Donnie Yen?
   B Yes, *it* / *you* is.
2. A Where *am* / *is* he from?
   B *He's* / *It's* from Hong Kong.
3. A *Am* / *Is* this restaurant good?
   B Yes! *He's* / *It's* great!
4. A She *'s not* / *'re not* from Britain. Where's she from?
   B *He's* / *She's* from Chile.
5. A Where *is* / *are* you from?
   B *I'm* / *It's* from Valletta.
6. A *Where's* / *Where are* Paris?
   B *It's* / *She's* in France.
7. A *Is* / *Are* that the Turkish flag?
   B No, it *is* / *'s not*.
8. A Spain's flag *am* / *is* red and yellow.
   B Yes, *I'm* / *you're* right.

2 ▶1.3 Complete the sentences. Listen and check.

1. I _____ from Peru.
2. Where _____ she from?
3. He _____ American; he's Canadian.
4. _____ you Elena?
5. This _____ Junko. She _____ from Japan.
6. I _____ not Argentinian.
7. You _____ from Argentina. _____ you from Chile?
8. I think he _____ from India.

VOCABULARY: Countries and nationalities

3 Complete the chart.

Country	Nationality
1_____	Canadian
Chile	2_____
China	3_____
France	4_____
5_____	German
6_____	Indian
Italy	7_____
Peru	8_____
Russia	9_____
10_____	British
the U.S.	11_____
Turkey	12_____

4 Complete the sentences with the correct country or nationality.

1. It's the flag of T*urke*y. (country)
2. It's the I*ndia*n flag. (nationality)

3. It's the S_____h flag.
4. It's the flag of C_____a.

5. It's the M_____n flag.
6. It's the C_____n flag.

7. It's the flag of B_____l.
8. It's the flag of the _____.

PRONUNCIATION: Word stress

5 ▶1.4 Is the stress on the nationality and country the same (S) or different (D)? Listen, check, and repeat.

1. Argentina — Argentinian — *S*
2. China — Chinese — *D*
3. Germany — German — ____
4. Italy — Italian — ____
5. Mexico — Mexican — ____
6. Turkey — Turkish — ____
7. Brazil — Brazilian — ____
8. Japan — Japanese — ____

Skills 1B

LISTENING: Listening for information about people

1 ▶ 1.5 Listen and complete the sentences with the words in the box.

addresses   countries   ~~first names~~
jobs   nationalities   numbers   last names

1 They are _first names_.
2 They are _____.
3 They are _____.
4 They are _____.
5 They are _____.
6 They are _____.
7 They are _____.

2 ▶ 1.6 Listen to two conversations. Where are the people?

3 ▶ 1.6 Listen again. Complete the forms.

	Student 1	Student 2
First name	1 _____	Yasin
Last name	Aleksandrov	5 _____
Nationality	2 _____	Turkish
Job	3 _____	6 _____
Classroom	4 _____	7 _____
Teacher	Sandrine	8 _____

4 ▶ 1.7 Listen and correct any contractions.

1 A What is his job?   _What's_
   B He is a student.   _He's_

2 A You are not from Argentina, are you?   _____
   B I am from Argentina!   _____

3 A It is not in classroom 8. It is in classroom 10.   _____
   B Where is that?   _____

4 A What is her nationality?   _____
   B She is from Canada.   _____

5 A You are a good singer!   _____
   B No, I am not.
   A You are!   _____

6 A I am in Shenzhen.   _____
   B Where is Shenzhen?   _____
   A It is in China.   _____

5 Look at the pictures and complete the job titles.

1 a _ _ _ _
2 e _ _ _ _ _ _ _ _
3 s _ _ _ _ _ _ _
4 I _   w _ _ _ _ _
5 r _ _ _ _ _ _ _
6 s _ _ _ _ _
7 s _ _ _ _ _
8 t _ _   g _ _ _ _
9 T _   h _ _ _ _
10 w _ _ _ _ _

1C LANGUAGE

GRAMMAR: The verb *be* (*we*, *you*, *they*)

1 Match sentences 1–10 with missing verbs a–c.

1 _____ the books expensive?
2 You and Harpinder _____ good friends.
3 Ursula, Frank, and the other students _____ in room 24.
4 _____ we in this classroom today?
5 They _____ sad; they are happy.
6 Liu and I _____ students from China.
7 You _____ a teacher. You're a student.
8 _____ you from Mexico?
9 We _____ the same age. He's 18 and I'm 20.
10 All the chefs here _____ Turkish.

　a are
　b 're not
　c Are

2 Look at the examples. Write sentences with pronouns.

1 her name = Marta
　It's Marta.
2 Keith and Sally ≠ American
　They're not American.
3 I ≠ a police officer
　_____
4 Pedro and Gabriela = from Brazil?
　_____
5 you and Aubert = happy?
　_____
6 you and I ≠ old.
　_____
7 Elena = 25
　_____
8 Michael = in Italy?
　_____
9 Yuki and Natsuki = from Japan
　_____
10 the book = interesting?
　_____

VOCABULARY: Numbers 11–100 and adjectives (1)

3 Write the words for the next two numbers in 1–6.

1 twelve, thirteen, fourteen,
　_____, _____ (15, 16)
2 twenty-four, twenty-six, twenty-eight,
　_____, _____ (30, 32)
3 one hundred, ninety, eighty,
　_____, _____ (70, 60)
4 eleven, twenty-two, thirty-three,
　_____, _____ (44, 55)
5 sixty-seven, seventy-three, seventy-nine,
　_____, _____ (85, 91)
6 ninety-nine, eighty-five, seventy-one,
　_____, _____ (57, 43)

4 ▶ 1.8 Complete the conversations with the correct adjectives. Listen and check.

1 **A** Are the shoes big?
　B No, they're very _____.
2 **A** That house is ugly.
　B Yes, it's not _____.
3 **A** Is he a _____ singer?
　B Yes. He's not bad.
4 **A** You don't look happy.
　B No, I'm not. I'm _____.
5 **A** The TV host is really boring!
　B Yes, she's not very _____.
6 **A** Is that watch $89? That's expensive!
　B Yes, it's not _____.
7 **A** This exercise is _____.
　B No it's not. It's easy.
8 **A** You're very _____, aren't you, Grandpa?
　B No, I'm not! I'm young!

PRONUNCIATION: Numbers

5 ▶ 1.9 Listen and choose the correct numbers.

1　13　　30
2　14　　40
3　15　　50
4　$16　$60
5　17　　70
6　18　　80
7　$19　$90
8　40　　42
9　52 km　62 km
10　83　　93

SKILLS 1D

WRITING: Filling out a form

1 Look at the picture and read the e-mail. Then fill out the form for Noemí.

2 Read the form. Then correct the capitals in the sentences below.

First name	Porfirio
Last name	Cubillos
Home city	Guadalajara
Nationality	Mexican
Country of residence	France
Married?	Yes
Wife's name	Claudine
Languages	Spanish, French, English

1 my name is porfirio cubillos.

2 i'm from guadalajara in mexico, but i am in france now.

3 my wife, claudine, is french.

4 at home, we speak spanish and french.

3 Write similar sentences for you. Remember to use capital letters correctly.

1 REVIEW and PRACTICE

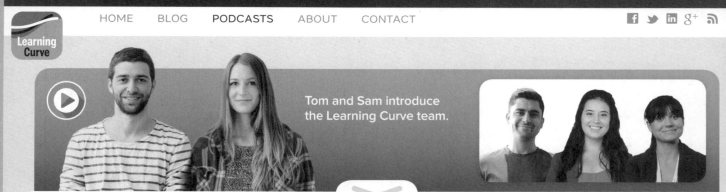

LISTENING

1 ▶ 1.10 Listen to the podcast about people at Learning Curve. In what order do the people speak? Write 1–5.

   a Jack _____
   b Penny _____
   c Tom _1_
   d Taylor _____
   e Sam _____

2 ▶ 1.10 Listen again. Match the people with the information.

   1 Tom _____   a is a chef.
   2 Sam _____   b is from the U.S.
   3 Taylor _____ c is a host of Learning Curve.
   4 Penny _____   d works with Tom.
   5 Jack _____   e is British and Argentinian.

3 ▶ 1.10 Listen again. Are the sentences true (T) or false (F)?

   1 Every episode of Learning Curve is about food or travel. _____
   2 Taylor also presents Learning Curve. _____
   3 Taylor is from the U.S. _____
   4 Penny lives in New York. _____
   5 Sam has a restaurant. _____
   6 Jack's last name is spelled G-O-O-D-E. _____

READING

1 Read Ethan's blog post about the city of Canberra. Match the people with photos a–c.

   1 Chia _____
   2 Bill _____
   3 Karen _____

2 Read the blog again. Check (✓) the correct sentences.

   1 Canberra is the capital of Australia. _____
   2 Canberra is an old city. _____
   3 Chia's family are Chinese. _____
   4 Chia is a doctor. _____
   5 Bill's wife is from Canberra. _____
   6 Houses in Canberra are cheap. _____
   7 Karen thinks downtown is ugly. _____
   8 It is easy to go from Canberra to the countryside. _____
   9 Karen doesn't like the weather in Australia. _____

3 Order the letters to make countries or nationalities. Write C or N.

   1 A N C H I _____
   2 N A P H I S S _____
   3 Y U T E R K _____
   4 C A R N E F _____
   5 I N D A N A C A _____
   6 U R S A S I _____
   7 M A N G E R _____
   8 A N P A J _____
   9 C E M I X O _____
   10 G I A N T A R E N _____

REVIEW and PRACTICE 1

HOME BLOG PODCASTS ABOUT CONTACT

Our guest blogger this week is Ethan. He's in Australia!

COOL CANBERRA!

This week's guest blogger Ethan Moore goes to a fantastic city "down under"*...

What is the capital city of Australia? Sydney? Melbourne perhaps? No, it's Canberra. Canberra's not big, like Sydney. And it's not as old as Melbourne. It's a new city, about a hundred years old. Its population is only 300,000 people. But it's a good city to live in. Three people who live here tell us why Canberra is so good.

Hi. My name's Chia. I love my city! My family is from China, but I'm Australian, too. Canberra is small, and the people are very friendly. It's great for shopping, and it's also very good for jobs. My friends all have good jobs here. They are doctors, receptionists, and IT workers. I'm an office worker – I work in a big building downtown. But it's only 15 minutes from my house.

Hello. I'm Bill and I'm 24. My wife and I are from Sydney. Sydney is a great city, but it's really expensive. A small house costs about $600,000! We can't afford that – I'm a teacher and my wife's a salesclerk. That's why we live in Canberra. It's not very cheap here, but it's less expensive than Sydney. Now we have a small house and we're very happy.

I'm Karen and I'm an engineer – hi! For me, Canberra is the perfect city because it's so beautiful. Downtown is very clean, and it's next to a big lake. You're never far from the countryside, and it's easy to get to – just ten minutes by car or on your bike! And of course the sky is blue, and the weather is perfect for being outside – it's Australia!

* If you go "down under", you go to Australia or New Zealand.

UNIT 2

People and things

2A LANGUAGE

GRAMMAR: Singular and plural nouns; *this*, *that*, *these*, *those*

1 Write the plural nouns.

1 She's a child.   They're _____.
2 It's a country.   They're _____.
3 It's a beach.   They're _____.
4 He's a person.   They're _____.
5 It's a nationality.   They're _____.
6 She's a waitress.   They're _____.
7 She's a woman.   They're _____.
8 It's a box.   They're _____.

2 ▶ 2.1 Look at the pictures. Complete the sentences with *this*, *that*, *these*, or *those*. Listen and check.

1 _____'s my doctor.

2 _____ is my backpack.

3 Are _____ your books?

4 Are _____ his pens?

5 Is _____ a dog?

6 _____ are beautiful dolls!

7 _____ is my house.

8 _____ are very old things.

VOCABULARY: Personal objects

3 Order the letters to make personal objects.

1 His money is in his L A W T E L.   _____
2 These S N A G L E S S U S are very expensive.   _____
3 You don't have any money? That's OK, you can pay by T R I C E D D R A C.   _____
4 I want to buy a small L E T B A T.   _____
5 Do you have a M A R E C A to take pictures?   _____
6 She keeps her keys in her S U P E R.   _____

4 Look at the pictures and complete the sentences.

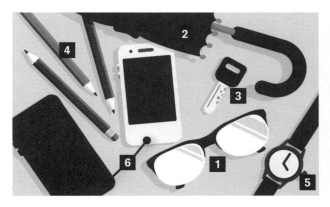

1 They're _____.
2 It's an _____.
3 It's a _____.
4 They're _____.
5 It's a _____.
6 They're _____.

PRONUNCIATION: /ɪ/ and /iy/

5 ▶ 2.2 Which words in 1–10 have the sound /ɪ/? Listen and check.

1 a three   b six
2 a listen   b read
3 a this   b these
4 a picture   b police
5 a he   b it
6 a engineer   b teacher
7 a pen   b credit card
8 a cheap   b expensive
9 a easy   b difficult
10 a keys   b pencil

SKILLS 2B

READING: Preparing to read

1 Complete the colors.

1 b _ _ _ k, b _ _ e, b _ _ _ n
2 g _ _ _ _ n, g _ _ y, g _ _ d
3 o _ _ _ _ e
4 p _ _ k, p _ _ _ _ e
5 r _ _
6 s _ _ _ _ r
7 w _ _ _ e
8 y _ _ _ _ w

2 Look at the text and the photos. Then choose the correct answers.

1 Where is the text from?
 a a website   c a newspaper
 b a letter
2 What does *prized* mean in the title?
 a expensive   c special
 b old
3 Who wrote the text?
 a one person   b more than one person

3 Read the text. Then read the sentences and write D (Danijela), M (Marko), C (Cheryl), or E (Eugenio).

1 This prized object is beautiful. _____
2 This person's object is big and goes everywhere with him or her. _____
3 These are expensive. _____
4 This object is from a grandparent. _____
5 His prized object is ugly. _____
6 His object helps him a lot. _____
7 Her prized object's old and new. _____
8 It's from his father and not small. _____

4 Complete the sentences with the words in the box.

very	ugly	prized	photos	old	object
it	is	isn't	glasses	family	expensive
earrings	difficult	beautiful	are		

1 Danijela says her _____ _____ _____.
2 Marko can't live without his _____ _____.
3 Cheryl loves her album full of _____ _____.
4 Eugenio loves the painting, but _____ _____ _____.
5 And you? What is your _____ _____?
6 This exercise _____ _____ _____. It's easy!

Our most prized objects

We all have objects we love for different reasons. Here are some people with their prized objects. And you? What's your special object?

Danijela, Slovenia

The important things in my life aren't objects; they're my friends and family. But I have a beautiful pair of earrings from my grandmother. They're not expensive, but I don't want to lose them.

Marko, Russia

I can't live without my glasses – they are my window to the world! Sometimes I can't find them, and it's difficult without them. They're a very expensive Italian pair. I've had these glasses for years, but they're still fantastic.

Cheryl, Philippines

My photo album is my most prized object. There are lots of family photos in it from when we were children. Some are twenty years old (they were my mother's), but I collected the photos in a new album last year. I take it with me everywhere.

Eugenio, Costa Rica

I love this painting of my great-grandfather (my grandfather's father). It's special because my father gave it to me. But my wife doesn't like it, and it's very big, so we don't have it in the house. It is a bit ugly, but I like it!

2C LANGUAGE

GRAMMAR: Possessive adjectives; 's for possession

1 Choose the correct words to complete the sentences.

1. Hi, *your / our / my* name's Nadya. Nice to meet you.
2. Rio de Janeiro is famous for *my / its / his* beaches.
3. That's Bozhi. He's a police officer. And that's *her / his / their* girlfriend with him.
4. We live in Sofia, but *our / your / its* home city is Varna.
5. And you? What's *my / her / your* name?
6. My parents live near the ocean. You can see it from *his / its / their* house.
7. What about you and your boyfriend? What are *your / his / my* jobs?
8. What's *our / your / her* job? Is she a doctor?
9. I'm a student. *Our / Their / My* classmates are great!
10. These are my dogs and that's *his / its / their* bed.

2 Complete the sentences. Use 's for possession.

1. He's the teacher. Those are his books.
   Those are **the teacher's** books.
2. This is my mother. That's her umbrella.
   That's my _____ umbrella.
3. She's Anna. That's her room.
   That's _____ room.
4. He's the tour guide. This is his camera.
   This is the _____ camera.
5. That's Hugo. This is his laptop.
   It's _____ laptop.
6. She's the engineer. Those are her keys.
   Those are the _____ keys.
7. That's my friend. This is his wallet.
   This is my _____ wallet.
8. He's the chef. That's his hat.
   That's the _____ hat.

VOCABULARY: Family and friends

3 Read the text and choose the correct options to complete the sentences.

Hi! I'm Tuyen. This is my family. Hung is my ¹ *daughter / husband / sister*, and we have two ² *children / daughters / sons*. Their names are Nhung and Vien. Nhung is six and her little ³ *brother / sister / son* is three. Vien has the same name as his ⁴ *grandmother / grandfather / husband*, my father, but we live with my husband's ⁵ *grandchildren / parents / wives*. Hung's ⁶ *father's / son's / husband's* name is Tuan and Tuan's ⁷ *daughter / sister / wife* is named Thu. They're wonderful, and it's great for the children to live with their ⁸ *grandfathers / grandparents / girlfriends*.

Kim, my husband's ⁹ *mother / sister / wife*, also lives with us. She's the photographer! She's not married, but she has a ¹⁰ *boyfriend / wife / husband*. His name's Chi.

(Photo labels: Tuan, Hung, Tuyen, Vien, Nhung, Thu)

4 Complete the sentences with the correct words.

1. Thu is Hung and Kim's _____.
2. Kim is Chi's _____.
3. Kim is Tuan and Thu's _____.
4. Thu is Nhung and Vien's _____.
5. Hung is Kim's _____.
6. Tuyen is Hung's _____.
7. Vien is Hung and Tuyen's _____.
8. Hung and Tuyen are Nhung and Vien's _____.

PRONUNCIATION: 's

5 ▶ 2.3 Say the sentences. Pay attention to the 's sound. Then listen, check, and repeat.

1. Is that George's mother?
2. They're Karina's sunglasses.
3. That watch is Haru's.
4. She's Pierre's sister.
5. Emma's cell phone is silver.
6. That's the doctor's son.

Skills 2D

SPEAKING: Telling the time

1 ▶ 2.4 Listen to the three conversations. Then choose the correct options to complete the sentences.

1 The time now is
   a nine ten.
   b nine thirty.
   c nine twenty.

2 The movie starts at
   a eight oh-five.
   b seven forty-five.
   c eight o'clock.

3 The meeting usually finishes at
   a seven thirty.
   b nine thirty.
   c ten o'clock.

2 ▶ 2.4 Listen again. What polite words do you hear? Check (✓) the words that you hear.

	Conversation		
	1	2	3
Excuse me	✓		
Please			
I'm sorry			
Thanks			
Thank you			

3 In which conversation in exercise 1 and 2 is the person not polite?

4 Read the answers and write the questions.

1 A What time/in Tokyo?
   _____
   B It's three a.m. there now.

2 A What time/train/to Boston?
   _____
   B It's in a half hour, at eleven ten.

3 A What time/your flight?
   _____
   B It's at six thirty.

4 A What time/now?
   _____
   B It's two forty-five.

5 A Excuse me, what/time?
   _____
   B I'm sorry, I don't know. I don't have a watch.

6 A What time/the class?
   _____
   B It's at five o'clock, in twenty minutes.

5 Order the words to make sentences. Then match them with questions a–d.

1 forty-five / four / is / it / p.m. / there
   _____

2 about / in / minutes / one / ten / there's
   _____

3 almost / is / it / o'clock / twelve / here
   _____

4 a.m. / at / it / on / opens / Saturdays / ten
   _____

a What time is the store open? ____
b What's the time? ____
c What time is it in Cairo? ____
d What time's the next bus downtown? ____

2 REVIEW and PRACTICE

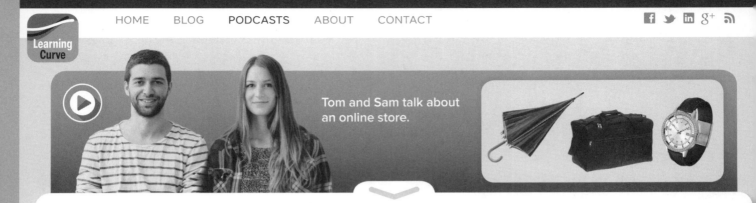

LISTENING

1 ▶ 2.5 Listen to the podcast about an online store called "yourfavoritethings.com". Check (✓) the things you hear.

- a watch _____
- b camera _____
- c tablet _____
- d sunglasses _____
- e pencils _____
- f keys _____
- g pen _____
- h umbrella _____
- i credit card _____
- j bag _____

2 ▶ 2.5 Listen again. Write T (true) or F (false).

1. Sam likes Tom's new watch. _____
2. Tom's watch is cheap. _____
3. Abbey's customers answer a lot of questions. _____
4. Abbey gives Tom a small box. _____
5. Tom lives in New York. _____
6. Tom goes to the gym. _____
7. Tom is never late. _____
8. Abbey's customers only pay for the things they like. _____
9. Tom likes Abbey's idea. _____
10. The umbrella in the box costs $50. _____

READING

1 Read Kate's blog about families. Choose the best summary for each person.

Selma
a Selma is unhappy because her parents are tired and poor.
b Selma is happy because she is going to college soon.
c Selma's family is not perfect, but she is happy.

Nicolás
a Nicolás is sad because his family has a small house and a small car.
b Nicolás likes being an only child because it's quiet and his family has money.
c Nicolás is happy because his parents are always out in the evenings.

2 Choose the correct options to complete the sentences.

1. Kate's parents have *two / three / four* children.
2. Selma's parents spend a lot of money on *games / food / clothes*.
3. Selma goes out with her *brothers / parents / sisters*.
4. Selma is sad about leaving her *brothers and sisters / parents / friends*.
5. Nicolás thinks his parents have a(n) *easy / difficult / boring* life.
6. Nicolás's parents spend a lot of money on *taxis / presents / sports*.
7. Nicolás goes out with his *parents / grandparents / cousins*.

REVIEW and PRACTICE 2

HOME BLOG PODCASTS ABOUT CONTACT

Our guest blogger this week is Kate.

BIG family or small family?

Are you from a big family or a small family? My family's not big and it's not small. I only have one brother and no sisters. Some families have a lot of children, and other families only have one child. But which are better – big families with all the fun and noise, or small families with peace and quiet? Let's hear from two people with very different families, Selma and Nicolás.

Selma: I have two brothers and three sisters, and we all live with our parents. I'm eighteen years old, and the others are seventeen, fourteen, eleven, seven, and two. I think my mother and father are very tired! Having two sons and four daughters is expensive for our parents, and they never have any money. I think it's because my brothers eat so much! Our parents only own one expensive thing – a very big car! But I think big families are great for the children. My brothers and sisters are my friends, and we are like a team. We argue and fight sometimes, but at the end of the day, we are a family. My sisters and I go out together, and my younger brothers and sisters always play together. And with so many brothers and sisters, life is never boring! I start college in Germany next year, and I'm sad about leaving them.

Nicolás: I am an only child and it's great. I think my parents are happy, too! We live in a small house and our car's not big, but that means we have more money to spend on other things. Every year we fly to Argentina to see my grandmother, and my parents have money to enjoy their life. My father plays golf every weekend, and my mother goes to classes with her friends in the evening. Their lives aren't difficult! They buy me a lot of expensive presents, too! And I never need a taxi to get home from parties because my father drives me everywhere! Sometimes I wish I had brothers and sisters to talk to. But I'm not alone – I have my girlfriend, my cousins, and my friends to go out with. And everything is calm and quiet in my family. Big families are so noisy!

UNIT 3 Food and drink

GRAMMAR: Simple present (I, you, we, they)

1 Choose the correct words to complete the conversations.

1. A *Do you like / Are you like / You do like* this book?
   B Yes, I *do / eat / like*.
2. A *Are / Be / Do* your friends play tennis?
   B *Do they play / They do play / They play* tennis every Sunday.
3. A Fruit cake? No, thanks. I *don't want / want / do want* it.
   B Oh, really? *Do I love / I do love / I love* fruit cake!
4. A *Am / Do / Is* that food good?
   B No, it's not. Well, I *am not like / don't like / like* it.
5. A Where *do want you / do you want / you do want* to go?
   B Nowhere, thanks. I *don't have / have / do have* enough time.
6. A *Do you / Are you / You do* know Maria?
   B No, but *do I / I don't / I* know her sister, Bella.

2 Rewrite the sentences. Use affirmative (+), negative (–), or question (?) forms.

1. I eat an apple every day.
   (–) *I don't eat an apple every day.*
2. We don't have class at eight o'clock.
   (+) _____
3. He is a taxi driver.
   (?) _____
4. Do they watch TV?
   (–) _____
5. They study English every day.
   (?) _____
6. Do you have a credit card?
   (+) _____
7. She is very happy.
   (–) _____
8. You speak Italian.
   (?) _____

VOCABULARY: Food and drink

3 Order the letters to make food and drink words.

1. Whole wheat D A B E R _____ W I N D C H A S E S _____ are good for you.
2. Does he drink O F F E C E _____ black or with L I K M _____?
3. Let's cook something quick like T A P S A _____.
4. I love the Z I P S A Z in Italy. _____.
5. Vegans don't eat T A M E _____ or S G E G _____.
6. Have some E T W A R _____ or A R N G O E C E I J U _____

4 Look at the photos and complete the crossword.

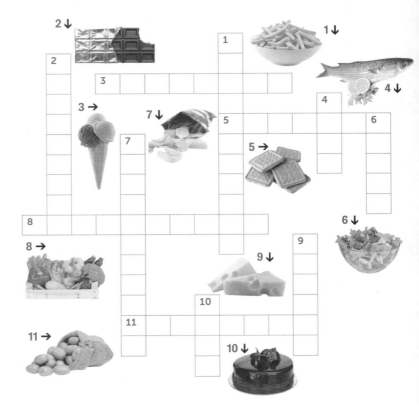

PRONUNCIATION: do you /dəyuw/

5 ▶ 3.1 Listen and complete the questions. Repeat the questions.

1. _____ potato chips?
2. _____ cake?
3. _____ Turkish food?
4. _____ milk in China?
5. _____ dinner?
6. _____ for breakfast?

SKILLS 3B

LISTENING: Listening for times and days

1 ▶ 3.2 Listen to the three conversations. Match the conversations with the places.

1 ____
2 ____
3 ____

a at a tourist information office
b at a train station
c at home
d in a restaurant
e in a store

2 ▶ 3.2 Listen again. Check (✓) the days and times you hear.

	Day		Time	
Conversation 1	Thursday ___	Friday ___	7:15 ___	7:50 ___
Conversation 2	Tuesday ___	Thursday ___	9:00 ___	7:00 p.m. ___
Conversation 3	Monday ___	Wednesday ___	2:15 p.m. ___	2:50 p.m. ___

3 ▶ 3.3 Listen to six conversations and complete the sentences.

1 One orange juice _____ two teas, please.
2 What day's good _____ you?
3 Please come _____ May 20th.
4 There's _____ bus _____ three thirty.
5 When _____ you want to meet _____ coffee?
6 Do you have _____ green bag?

4 Complete the calendar with the correct words.

	¹y e s t e r d a y	today	²_____		Week Month Year
	³M ____	⁴T _____	⁵W _____	⁶T _____	⁷F _____	the ⁸w _____ (Saturday and ⁹S _____)
6:00 a.m.–12:00 p.m.	in the morning		8:00 a.m. play tennis with Marina			
12:00 p.m.–5:00 p.m.	in the ¹⁰a _____		1:30 p.m. have lunch - Gustozo's			
5:00 p.m.–10:00 p.m.	in the ¹¹e _____		6:00–9:00 p.m. study for exam			
10:00 p.m.–12:00 a.m.	at ¹²n ____		10:00 p.m. call James			

17

3C LANGUAGE

GRAMMAR: Simple present (he, she, it)

1 Order the words to make sentences. Write the correct capital letters.

1 **A** Ciudad Juárez / does / Gabi / in / live
_____?
B No, she doesn't. lives / Monterrey / in / she
_____.

2 **A** does / Lionel / study / where
_____?
B goes / he / the University of Chicago / to
_____.

3 **A** doesn't / have / any money / Naomi
_____.
B does / some today / need / she
_____?

4 **A** doesn't / your / phone / why / work
_____?
B I don't know. anything / do / doesn't / it
_____.

5 **A** on the weekend / does / Halcon / sports / watch
_____?
B Yes. he / likes watching / rugby / tennis and
_____.

2 Complete the sentences with the verbs in the correct form of the simple present.

1 Giovanna _____ (not go) to work until 7 o'clock.
2 Alex _____ (watch) TV all day on Sundays!
3 _____ (Yannick exchange) some money before he travels?
4 This watch _____ (not work). It's very old.
5 Issam _____ (speak) to his parents every weekend.
6 Cathy is busy on Saturdays. She _____ (study) in the morning.
7 _____ (Elena exercise) much?
8 _____ (Nils want) the pasta or a pizza?
9 Her husband _____ (not like) tea or coffee.
10 _____ (you have) a car or a bike?

VOCABULARY: Common verbs (1)

3 Match the two parts of the sentences.

1 Do you want _____
2 I go _____
3 We live in _____
4 I don't know the _____
5 Oliver, say _____
6 On Friday evenings, we watch _____
7 I don't work _____
8 She studies _____

a answer. Do you?
b coffee or a cold drink?
c a house, not an apartment.
d to school by train.
e a movie, either a DVD or on the Internet.
f goodbye to your grandmother.
g Japanese as a hobby.
h in an office.

4 Complete the sentences with the correct verbs.

1 Do you _____ to high school or college?
2 He doesn't want to _____ TV all day.
3 Most people _____ a computer these days.
4 My brother and sister _____ lunch for the family on weekends.
5 She doesn't _____ many sports except basketball.
6 We _____ a black-and-white cat called "Pudding."

PRONUNCIATION: -s and -es endings

5 ▶ 3.4 Put the verbs in the correct column. Then listen and check.

| changes | ~~eats~~ | goes | knows | lives |
| makes | uses | watches | works | |

/s/	/z/	/ɪz/
eats	_____	_____
_____	_____	_____
_____	_____	_____

SKILLS 3D

WRITING: Punctuation

1 Read the blog and choose the correct photo (a, b, or c).

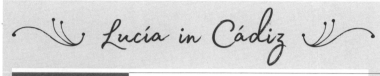
Lucía in Cádiz

| ABOUT | LATEST POST | CONTACT |

Hello! My name's Lucía. This blog is all about my city, Cádiz in Spain.

☆ Carnival! ☆☆☆☆☆☆☆☆☆

It's February, and every year at this time, we celebrate Carnival, a time for singing, eating, and friends. There's lots to talk about – the singing competition, the costumes, the people, etc. – but in this post, I want to tell you about the food.

Insert photo here

People buy food and eat it in the street. Cádiz is next to the ocean, and it is famous for its seafood: fish and other things from the ocean. In the photo, you can see *erizos*. They are ugly but I love them! But my favorite food during Carnival are the sweet cookies called *pestiños*. They're not good for you, but they're delicious!

a

b

c

2 Rewrite the sentences with the correct punctuation and capital letters.

1 Lucía is from spain.
_____

2 Carnival's not in February.
_____

3 During Carnival, people like singing eating and seeing their friends
_____

4 people don't usually eat food in restaurants during Carnival.
_____

5 lucía thinks *erizos* are beautiful.
_____

6 Lucía's favorite food's not good for you?
_____

3 Are the sentences in exercise 2 true or false? Write T or F.

1 ___   3 ___   5 ___
2 ___   4 ___   6 ___

4 Match the two parts of the sentences.

1 She likes ice cream, but ___
2 My grandfather is pretty old, but ___
3 Sandra shops at the grocery store, but ___
4 I work in a big office and ___
5 The festival is called New Year, but ___
6 Frida has a good job and ___

a he still plays sports.
b we buy vegetables at the market.
c I love it!
d she's very happy.
e it's not on January 1st.
f her brother prefers fruit.

5 Write a plan for a blog post about a family celebration in your house, e.g. a birthday or holiday. Answer these questions.

- When is the celebration and why do you celebrate it?
- What do you do on the day?
- What special food do you have?
- What's your favorite part of the celebration?

6 Write your blog post. Remember to:

- use correct punctuation and capital letters.
- use the linkers *and* and *but*.

3 REVIEW and PRACTICE

LISTENING

1 ▶ 3.5 Listen to the podcast about "morning people" and "evening people." For each of the people Sam interviews (1–4), write MP (morning person), EP (evening person), or B (both).

1 _____
2 _____
3 _____
4 _____

2 ▶ 3.5 Listen again. Complete each sentence with one word from the podcast.

1 Sam thinks Tom is an _____ person.
2 Sam asked four different people the _____ question yesterday.
3 Speaker 1 is an _____.
4 Speaker 1 works every _____.
5 Speaker 2 is a _____.
6 Speaker 2's _____ sleep in the morning.
7 Speaker 3 works in a _____.
8 Speaker 3 sometimes sleeps in a quiet _____.
9 Speaker 4 works during the _____.
10 Speaker 4 says _____ are expensive at night.

READING

1 Read Jack's blog about cooking. Match paragraphs 1–4 with photos a–d.

1 ___
2 ___
3 ___
4 ___

2 Read the blog again. Choose the correct answers.

1 The food Jack likes is _____.
   a expensive and difficult to cook
   b expensive and easy to cook
   c cheap and easy to cook

2 Jack says people can _____ for quick recipes.
   a look in a book
   b look on the Internet
   c ask a chef

3 Jack says a simple pasta dish can take _____ to cook.
   a ten minutes
   b 30 minutes
   c three hours

4 Jack says chefs _____ learning to cook.
   a don't spend a long time
   b spend a long time
   c don't like

5 Jack says _____ aren't expensive.
   a meat and fish
   b vegetables
   c pasta and tomatoes

6 Jack thinks the best thing people can do is _____.
   a buy food from a store
   b buy food from other countries
   c grow their own food

7 Jack says food that _____ can be bad for the planet.
   a is expensive
   b comes from other countries
   c is difficult to cook

HOME BLOG PODCASTS ABOUT CONTACT

Our guest blogger this week is Jack.

KEEP IT simple

Many people think all the best meals are very expensive and difficult to cook. But it's just not true! Most of my favorite dishes are very easy to make, and cheap, too! Let's look at four ways to make cooking cheap and easy, and why it's important.

a — Grown your own!

1 It's true that many of the most famous dishes in good restaurants take a long time to cook. In fact, sometimes chefs start a meal days before they serve it! But most people don't have three hours to cook a meal every evening. The good news is there are hundreds of quick recipes online – meals that take less than 30 minutes from start to finish. For a very quick meal, a plate of pasta and tomato sauce only takes ten minutes!

b — Think local!

2 Chefs study how to cook for years, and we can do a lot of different things in the kitchen. But some of my favorite dishes are very, very simple. A piece of fish with some fresh vegetables is delicious, and really easy to cook. Because it only uses a few ingredients, the taste is clean and fresh.

c — Simple to make!

3 In many restaurants, you spend a lot of money to have a nice meal. But good food isn't always expensive. In most countries, good meat and fish is expensive, but vegetables are cheap. And food from other countries often costs a lot of money. It's better to buy food from your own country. Or even better, grow your own food!

d — Start early!

4 Cheap, simple, local food is good for you and it's good for the planet. Food from other countries often travels hundreds of miles by airplane. This is bad for everyone. That's another reason to use food from near where you live.

Go to my website for lots of cheap and easy recipes. Or come to my restaurant and let me cook for you!

UNIT 4

Daily life

4A LANGUAGE

GRAMMAR: Frequency adverbs

1 Choose the correct place in each sentence for the adverb in parentheses: (a), (b), or (c).

1 I (a) have (b) lunch (c) at 1 o'clock. (*usually*)
2 (a) He (b) drinks hot milk (c). (*never*)
3 That store (a) has (b) expensive sunglasses (c) and cheap ones. (*often*)
4 We (a) watch (b) a movie on Friday night (c). (*always*)
5 My sister and I (a) do (b) our homework (c) together. (*sometimes*)
6 Engineers (a) use (b) a computer (c) all day. (*often*)
7 (a) They (b) leave class (c) early. (*never*)
8 (a) Marco (b) comes (c) late to work! (*always*)

2 Look at the calendar. Then complete the sentences about Shruthi's day. Use adverbs of frequency.

Monday	Tuesday	Wednesday	Thursday	Friday
6:30 a.m. play sports	6:30 a.m. play sports	6:30 a.m. play sports	6:45 a.m. play sports	6:30 a.m. play sports
7:45 a.m. have breakfast with Ana	7:45 a.m. have breakfast with Ana	7:45 a.m. have breakfast with Ana		7:45 a.m. have breakfast with Ana
8:30–6.00 work	8:30–6:30 work	8.30–6.00 work	8:30–6:30 work	8:30–6:00 work
	1:00 p.m. go to Mario's restaurant		1:30 p.m. go to Brown's restaurant	1:00 p.m. go to El Toro restaurant
6:00 p.m. leave work	6:30 p.m. leave work	6:00 p.m. leave work	6:30 p.m. leave work	6:00 p.m. leave work
6:30 p.m. study Japanese	7:00 p.m. study Japanese		7:00 p.m. study Japanese	
7:30 p.m. watch TV	9:30 p.m. watch TV	8:45 p.m. watch TV	9:00 p.m. watch TV	8:00 p.m. see movie at the movie theater

1 Shruthi ___*always plays sports*___ before 7:00 a.m.
2 She _____ breakfast with Ana.
3 She _____ from eight thirty.
4 She _____ to a restaurant for lunch.
5 She _____ work before 6:00 p.m.
6 She _____ studies Japanese after work.
7 She _____ a movie at the movie theater.
8 She _____ TV in the evenings.

VOCABULARY: Daily routine verbs

3 Order the letters to make daily routine verbs.

I'm a chef, so I have a long day. I [1] *teg pu* _____ at seven o'clock and wake my children up. After I [2] *teg ddeerss* _____, I make breakfast. Mornings are the only time I see the children. We [3] *aeelv ehmo* _____ at eight thirty – I don't [4] *arstt korw* _____ until eleven, but I take the children to school before that. My job is difficult and I don't [5] *fiihns krow* _____ until eleven o'clock! I always [6] *ekta a ehrosw* _____ before I [7] *og ot bde* _____ at night.

4 Look at the pictures. Complete the sentences with daily routine verbs.

1 She _____ to music when she's on the bus.
2 I usually _____ in the mornings.

3 We _____ together in our bedroom.
4 He _____ late in the evening.

5 They _____ at the mall every Sunday.
6 Do you _____ when you go to bed?

PRONUNCIATION: Sentence stress

5 ▶ 4.1 Listen to the sentences. Pay attention to the sentence stress. Listen again and repeat.

1 I never have breakfast at a café.
2 He sometimes studies on the weekend.
3 It's often cold here at night.
4 They usually eat salad with lunch.
5 We always watch TV on the computer.
6 She never says "thank you."

SKILLS 4B

READING: Finding specific information

1 Complete the sentences with transportation words.

1 This is another word for *underground train* or *metro*. _____
2 This goes very fast, like a car, but has two wheels. _____
3 This is like a boat, goes on water, and is usually very big. _____
4 You can pay someone to drive you in this car. _____
5 This is big and lots of people pay to go to work on the road in it. _____
6 This has two wheels and you can ride it for exercise. _____
7 You can travel by air to other countries in this. _____
8 This is big, it doesn't go on the road, and you pay to travel in it. _____

2 Read the article about five people's trips. Match each person with the correct transportation. You can use more than one letter.

1 Giovanna _____
2 Jiang _____
3 Lupita _____
4 Gary _____
5 Henry _____

a bike
b bus
c ferry
d on foot
e plane
f the subway

3 Read the article again. Choose the correct options to complete the sentences. Where in the text is the information?

1 The article is about people's *favorite / difficult / daily* trips.
2 The *vaporetto* is a *plane / ferry / train*.
3 Jiang travels for *30 minutes / two and a half hours / five hours* every day.
4 It's difficult for Lupita to *study at home / go to school / get home*.
5 In some parts of Australia, doctors travel by *boat / motorbike / plane*.
6 Henry goes by bike because it is *cheap / clean / fast*.

4 Complete the sentences with a person's name or a place from the article. Then choose P for possession or C for contraction.

1 _____'s Australian. P C
2 Singapore, _____'s city, is perfect for bikes. P C
3 _____'s job is in Venice. P C
4 _____'s a high school student. P C
5 The college in Nanjing is not near _____'s home. P C
6 Giovanna uses _____'s public transportation. P C

It's not always easy to get to the place you want. Many people study or work far from their homes. Here are five people with interesting daily trips.

Giovanna is a tour guide in Venice, Italy. Like many people, she travels around by *vaporetto*, the local "bus" service... except in Venice, these buses don't go on the road, they are ferries! "I love my trip to work," she says.

Jiang studies in Nanjing, China. His college is a long way from home. He takes two buses, the subway, and then walks for 30 minutes. The total time for his trip? Two and a half hours each way!

Lupita's house is in the mountains in Colombia, but her high school is a long way down the mountain. She goes on foot. "Going to school is easy," she says, "but getting home is very difficult!"

Gary is one of Australia's "flying doctors." He often travels long distances to see his patients, sometimes hundreds of miles. How? By plane!

Henry gets everywhere really fast in his city, Singapore. "This is the perfect city to use a bike," he says. "It's so safe and easy."

4C LANGUAGE

GRAMMAR: Simple present: *wh-* questions

1 Match questions 1–9 with answers a–i. Then complete the questions with the words in the box.

how	how many	how old	what
what time	when	where	who	why

1 _How many_ brothers and sisters do you have? _e_
2 _____ do people here do on weekends? ____
3 _____ is Greta happy? ____
4 _____ does the class start? ____
5 _____ is he? ____
6 _____ do your parents live? ____
7 _____ is that girl on the TV? ____
8 _____ do they get to work? ____
9 _____ is her birthday? ____

a At 9:45, I think.
b They go on the subway.
c It's next Tuesday.
d She's a singer.
e I have two sisters.
f In a beautiful place called Puebla.
g Most people go to the beach.
h He's three today!
i Because she has a new job.

2 Order the words to make questions. Add *do*, *does*, *am*, *is*, or *are*.

1 movie / what / your favorite
   _____?
2 how / know / the answer / they
   _____?
3 by car / Casey / go / to school / why
   _____?
4 old / your mother / how
   _____?
5 finish / Jerry / time / what / work
   _____?
6 glasses / my / where
   _____?
7 how / you live / many / people / with
   _____?
8 the teacher / this / morning / where
   _____?
9 get / home / when / your / brother
   _____?
10 in the class / know / who / you
   _____?

VOCABULARY: Adjectives (2)

3 ▶ 4.2 Complete the conversations with a pair of words in the box in the correct order. Listen and check.

clean/dirty	cold/hot	long/short
horrible/nice	noisy/quiet	

1 A Is it _____ in here?
   B No, it's only 55 °F. I'm pretty _____.
2 A You're very _____! I want to listen to the radio.
   B I'm sorry, Mom. I'll be _____.
3 A I don't want to watch a _____ movie. It's late.
   B OK. This movie is very _____ – only 80 minutes.
4 A Is the city _____?
   B No! It's _____. I don't like the noise and the traffic!
5 A I'm very _____ from doing housework.
   B Yes, now the house is _____, but you're not! Take a shower!

4 Complete each sentence with the correct adjective.

1 Buy a s _ _ _ _ cake, not a big one, because not many people know about the party.
2 I love Mexico. It's interesting and the people are very f _ _ _ _ _ _.
3 It takes six hours to get to the city on the s _ _ _ train, but the tickets are cheap.
4 New electric cars are quiet and they are also f _ _ _.
5 Our hotel room is fantastic. It has a really l _ _ _ _ bed.
6 We never go to that grocery store – the salesclerks are so u _ _ _ _ _ _ _ _!

PRONUNCIATION: Question words

5 ▶ 4.3 Listen to the questions. Are *do* and *does* stressed? Listen again, check, and repeat.

1 When do you listen to the radio?
2 What books does he read?
3 How many movies do they watch each week?
4 Who does she go to the movies with?
5 Why do you like shopping?
6 What time do you study?

SKILLS **4D**

SPEAKING: Shopping for food

1 ▶ 4.4 Look at the pictures and listen to a customer in a store. Does the customer buy a, b, or c?

2 ▶ 4.4 Choose the correct options to complete the conversation. Then listen again and check.

1 How ____ I help you?
  a do   b can   c am
2 Do ____ have fruit juice?
  a you   b I   c we
3 ____ I have orange juice, please?
  a Do   b Am   c Can
4 How ____ is that?
  a much   b many   c more
5 I'd ____ some of that, please.
  a want   b like   c have
6 Here you are. ____ else?
  a Nothing   b Something c Anything
7 ____ thirteen dollars and twenty-five cents.
  a That's   b This is   c Here's
8 Here ____ go.
  a I   b you   c they
9 And ____ your change.
  a it's   b here's   c where's

3 ▶ 4.5 Look at the photos and listen to three conversations. Match the conversations (1–3) with the photos (a–c).

1 ____ 2 ____ 3 ____

4 ▶ 4.5 Listen to the three conversations again. Write 1, 2, or 3.

a The customer and the salesclerk are polite. ____
b The customer is <u>not</u> polite. ____
c The salesclerk is <u>not</u> polite. ____

25

4 REVIEW and PRACTICE

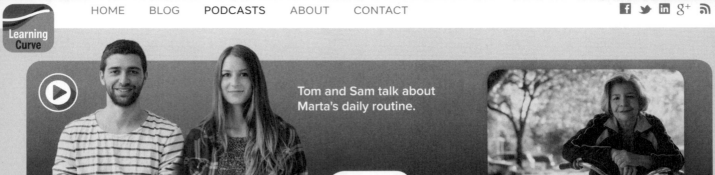

LISTENING

1 ▶ 4.6 Listen to the podcast about a person's daily routine. Check (✓) the verbs you hear.

a get up _____
b take a shower _____
c get dressed _____
d have breakfast _____
e do housework _____
f leave home _____
g start work _____
h finish work _____
i get home _____
j do homework _____

2 ▶ 4.6 Listen again and choose the correct answers.

1 Where is Marta from?
 a France
 b Brazil
 c Spain
2 What time does Marta's day start?
 a 5:00
 b 5:15
 c 5:30
3 How does Marta travel to her daughter's house?
 a on the subway
 b by bike
 c by car
4 How far is Marta's house from her daughter's house?
 a five miles
 b ten miles
 c fifteen miles
5 What time does Marta's daughter arrive home?
 a 6:00
 b 6:30
 c 8:30
6 What does Marta do before she goes to bed?
 a She cooks a meal.
 b She watches TV.
 c She reads a book.

READING

1 Read Penny's blog about a long trip. How many types of transportation does José tell her about?

a eight
b nine
c ten

2 Read the blog again. Write Y (Yes) or N (No).

1 Penny's family doesn't like her travel plans. _____
2 José is Chilean. _____
3 The bus from Lima to Cusco is expensive. _____
4 The trip to Machu Picchu by car is easy. _____
5 Most people go to La Paz by bike. _____
6 José thinks the people in La Paz are nice. _____
7 Walking tours in Santiago are cheap. _____
8 Buenos Aires is a good city to see on foot. _____

3 Match the adjectives with their opposites.

1 cold _____   a unfriendly
2 noisy _____   b quiet
3 fast _____   c horrible
4 friendly _____   d cold
5 long _____   e hot
6 nice _____   f dirty
7 clean _____   g slow
8 hot _____   h short

REVIEW and PRACTICE 4

HOME **BLOG** PODCASTS ABOUT CONTACT

Guest blogger Penny tells us about her latest travel plans.

A long trip

"It's a very bad idea." That's what everyone says when I tell them my travel plans. And this is what my friends and family say when I tell them my new idea – to spend one month traveling from Lima in Peru to Buenos Aires in Argentina. "It's dangerous!" says my mother. "It's expensive!" says my father. "It's really hot!" says one friend. "It's really cold!" says another friend. Maybe they're right, but there is one thing I know – it's going to be an exciting trip!

It's a long trip and I don't want to be in a bus or car for a month. My plan is to use different types of transportation on my trip. My friend José is from Mexico, but he knows Peru and Chile very well. So, I asked him for help and he sent me this information. Thanks José!

OK, Penny, you start your adventure in Lima. It's about seven hours from New York by plane. From Lima you go to the town of Cusco by bus. The bus is noisy and it's not fast, but it's cheap. And there are beds! Cusco is famous because it's near Machu Picchu. The best way to get to Machu Picchu from Cusco is by train and then on foot. It is possible to go by car but don't – the roads are very bad! After Machu Picchu, take the train back to Cusco and your next stop is La Paz, in Bolivia.

Most people travel to La Paz by bus, but why don't you go by bike? You go around the beautiful Lake Titicaca. Stop for a day and see the lake by boat – it's an amazing place! Seven more days on your bike and you arrive in La Paz. Spend two or three days in La Paz because it's a very interesting city with friendly people.

I have an idea for the trip to Santiago in Chile – go by motorcycle! It's a long trip (about four days), but the views are great. Santiago is another interesting city, and the best way to see it is on foot. There are walking tours and they're not expensive.

Your final trip is by train from Santiago to Buenos Aires. It's a long trip so go to the city of Mendoza by bus. Then take a different bus to Buenos Aires. The buses in Chile and Argentina are cheap and clean. Buenos Aires is a great city, but it is very big to see on foot. Travel on the subway to see everything.

What an exciting trip. Have fun!

All about me

5A LANGUAGE

GRAMMAR: *can* and *can't*

1 Complete the sentences and questions with *can*, *can't*, and the verbs in the box.

> take   eat   read   start   study   ~~watch~~

1 A ___Can___ we ___watch___ a movie?
   B No, you ___can't___!

2 A I _____ _____ work at seven a.m. No problem.
   B That's great!

3 A _____ I _____ a shower?
   B Yes, you _____!

4 A He's only three, but he _____ _____ books.
   B That's amazing!

5 A What's the problem?
   B It's very noisy! I _____ _____ in here!

6 A _____ your dog _____ chocolate?
   B No, he _____, it's bad for him.

2 Complete the conversations. Use *can* or *can't* and any other words you need.

1 "It's my brother's birthday tomorrow." "Really? I _____ a cake for him!"

2 "Can you speak Russian, Dominic?" "Yes, _____. Why? Is that an e-mail from your Russian friend?"

3 "Emma says she knows about computers, but she _____ her new tablet." "I'm sure she _____. We _____ help her. It's easy!"

4 "We have some dollars, but we need euros in Paris. _____ some money at that bank?" "No, _____. The bank's not open today."

5 "My grandfather is very old, but he _____ a newspaper without glasses." "_____ a car without them?"

6 "Can Sheila go shopping today?" "No, _____."

VOCABULARY: Common verbs (2)

3 Choose the correct verbs to complete the sentences.

I ¹ *call / speak / travel* my grandmother every day, but on Wednesdays and Fridays, I go to her house to ² *arrive / give / look after* her because she can't ³ *cook / give / help* her own lunch. Sometimes my sister ⁴ *speaks / helps / calls* me, but I usually do it alone. My grandmother sometimes ⁵ *dances / plays / sings* the piano for me. She also likes to get out of the house, so I often ⁶ *drive / arrive / travel* her to the ocean. She loves to ⁷ *call / travel / swim* in the ocean. On weekends, she sometimes ⁸ *helps / meets / sings* her friends for coffee.

4 Complete each pair of sentences with the same verb in the correct form.

1 A You must _____ at the airport two hours before your flight.
   B He always _____ late.

2 A She doesn't _____ salsa, but she's good at ballet.
   B I love this band! Do you want to _____ with me?

3 A My French isn't very good, but I can _____ Spanish.
   B Do you often _____ to your brothers?

4 A I _____ to different countries for my job.
   B It's easy to _____ to the city by train.

5 A Do the students _____ presents to their teachers?
   B He never _____ me back my pen after class!

6 A I can't _____, but I love listening to music.
   B It's a very difficult song to _____.

7 A The ocean's too cold to _____ in today.
   B I sometimes _____ in the pool in town.

PRONUNCIATION: *can* and *can't*

5 ▶ 5.1 Listen to the sentences. Write affirmative (+), negative (−), or question (?). Listen again, check, and repeat.

1 _____   5 _____
2 _____   6 _____
3 _____   7 _____
4 _____   8 _____

28

SKILLS 5B

LISTENING: Listening for specific information

1 Match sentences 1–6 with the pairs of photos a–f. Then complete the words with the missing vowels (a, e, i, o, u).

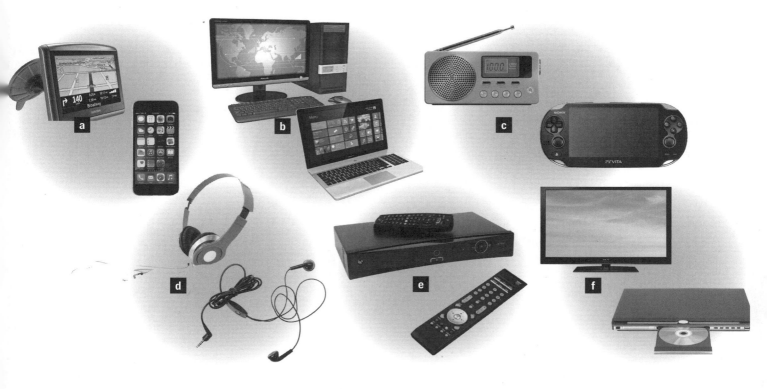

1 I don't have a d__skt__p c__mp__t__r. I have a l__pt__p.
2 Many people watch movies on t__l__v__s__ __n from the Internet but some also have DVD pl__y__rs.
3 I can't use __ __rph__n__s, so I use h__ __dph__n__s to listen to music.
4 There's no need for a GPS in your car if you own a sm__rtph__n__.
5 I play v__d__ __g__m__s or listen to the r__d__ __ on the bus.
6 This r__m__t__ c__ntr__l is for the DVR – the "d__g__t__l v__d__ __ r__c__rd__r."

2 ▶5.2 Listen to a radio show about technology. Choose the best title, a, b, or c.

a Three reasons why people don't use technology.
b Three electronic devices people use.
c Three people with technology problems.

3 Read the sentences. Are the missing words a person, place, number, or thing?

1 The speaker uses electronic technology for about ___number___ hours each day.
2 The speaker's _____ doesn't need a cell phone.
3 A family can use the Internet in _____ or more ways, with different electronic devices.
4 Some people think that the _____ is not safe.
5 They think that big Internet companies want our personal _____.
6 People in the _____ look at screens for about twelve hours every day.

4 ▶5.2 Listen again and complete the sentences in exercise 3.

5 ▶5.3 Read the sentences and underline the important words. Then listen, check, and repeat.

1 My family comes from China, but I live in Japan.
2 I can't buy the black laptop because it's too expensive.
3 That tablet is my sister's, not mine.
4 I study Spanish, so I listen to Spanish radio online.

6 ▶5.4 Listen and write the important words.

1 I usually _____ _____ on my _____ before I _____ to _____.
2 Craig _____ _____ to _____ in his _____.
3 It says on the _____ that the _____ _____ at _____ o'clock.

5C LANGUAGE

GRAMMAR: Object pronouns

1 Choose the correct pronouns to complete the text.

Hi! My name's Gabriela, but I don't like ¹ *her / it / she*, so people call me Gabi. I'm 20 years old, and I'm a college student. There are lots of young people there, but I'm not like most of ² *him / them / they*. They like dancing and enjoying themselves in the evening, but those things aren't fun for ³ *it / me / them*. I love sports, and I play ⁴ *them / they / us* with my friends, Piotr and Maggie. Piotr enjoys going out on his bike, so I often go bike riding with ⁵ *he / her / him*. Maggie loves swimming, so I go with ⁶ *her / it / she* to the swimming pool every Tuesday. Why do we like exercising? Because it's good for ⁷ *it / us / we*, and we're happy when we do ⁸ *it / them / him*. What about ⁹ *her / us / you*? Do you enjoy sports or do you hate ¹⁰ *him / them / me*?

2 Complete each sentence with one object pronoun and one subject pronoun.

1 Can I have your pen? I only need _____ for a minute. Oh, no, _____'s red! I need a black one.
2 _____ don't speak Portuguese well, but my friend João teaches _____ every week.
3 Evgeny and I like the same music. _____ normally listen to rap and R&B. Katerina likes the same music as _____.
4 Excuse me, are _____ OK? Can I help _____?
5 I go to the gym with Jamie. _____ takes me in her car. It's very nice of _____.
6 Lali and Naomi don't like the beach. It's too hot for _____ and _____ can't swim.
7 Michel studies English with me. _____'s from Vietnam. I often see _____ after school.
8 Patricia is an actress. I sometimes see _____ on television, but _____'s not very famous.

VOCABULARY: Activities

3 ▶ 5.5 Listen and write the activities.

Jobs in the house	Sports
1 _____	3 _____
2 _____	4 _____

Evenings and weekends	Activities on your own
5 _____	7 _____
6 _____	_____
_____	8 _____

4 Complete each sentence with an activity.

1 She loves _____, but she doesn't have a bike!
2 _____ magazines is a great way to learn a new language.
3 There's no food in the house. We need to do some _____ _____ today.
4 _____ in the ocean is very cold in some _____ _____ countries!
5 I don't enjoy _____ at the movie theater, but I like them on TV.
6 They're not good at _____ to disco music, but they like watching other people do it.

PRONUNCIATION: /h/

5 ▶ 5.6 Listen. Pay attention to the sound /h/. Listen again and repeat.

1 **A** How's your homework?
   B It's hard!
2 **A** He has lots of housework.
   B Doesn't Hillary help?
3 **A** Is her husband happy?
   B No, he hates his job.
4 **A** Hello. How is your vacation?
   B It's very hot!
5 **A** Are those his headphones?
   B No, they're Heidi's.
6 **A** When does Harry leave home?
   B At eight thirty.

SKILLS 5D

WRITING: Describing yourself

1 Read Margarita's profile. Which questions (1–7) does it answer? Write the paragraphs (a–d).

1 How do you travel around the city? ____
2 Where do you live? ____
3 What do you like doing in your free time? ____
4 What do you like watching on TV? ____
5 What job do you do? ____
6 What do you like to eat? ____
7 What jobs does your family do? ____

a Hi! My name's Margarita, but you can call me Marga. I'm a police officer. It's an interesting job ¹ ____.

b I live in Recife, a city in the north of Brazil. Many tourists visit Recife ² ____. I live downtown in an apartment with my friend Camila.

c In my free time I like reading and cooking. I go running, but I don't like it much ³ ____. But I love swimming. Recife has a great beach, so I go there two or three times a week.

d My family is from Recife. They live near me. I have two brothers and a little sister. My sister is in college. She studies IT ⁴ ____. My father and one of my brothers are police officers, like me. My other brother is a really good chef in an expensive restaurant, but he doesn't do the cooking when we are all together at home ⁵ ____!

2 Match reasons a–g with blanks 1–5 in the profile. There are two extra reasons.

a because he thinks home cooking is too easy ____
b because I meet lots of different people and help them with their problems ____
c because the people are unfriendly ____
d because it's boring ____
e because she wants to be a computer programmer ____
f because I can't drive ____
g because it's a beautiful place near the ocean ____

3 Write a personal profile for someone in your family, a friend, or a famous person. Make sure you:

- answer some of the questions in exercise 1.
- use paragraphs.
- give reasons with *because*.

5 REVIEW and PRACTICE

HOME BLOG PODCASTS ABOUT CONTACT

Tom and Sam talk to four people about things they can't do.

LISTENING

1 ▶ 5.7 Listen to the podcast about things people can't do. Complete each sentence with one or two words.

1 Lorenzo can't _____.
2 Beatrice can't _____.
3 Zoe can't _____.
4 Roberto can't _____.

2 ▶ 5.7 Listen again. Choose T (true) or F (false).

1 Sam thinks she can cook.   T / F
2 Lorenzo doesn't have a car.   T / F
3 Lorenzo's friends never go to the beach.   T / F
4 Beatrice can't dance.   T / F
5 Zoe's daughter can swim.   T / F
6 Zoe wants to learn how to swim.   T / F
7 Roberto can speak Spanish.   T / F
8 Roberto wants a Portuguese teacher.   T / F

3 Write the common verbs.

1 Can you p_____ any musical instruments?
2 Let's m_____ this afternoon outside school.
3 I can dance well, but I can't s_____ at all!
4 When you get home this evening, c_____ me.
5 Which countries do you want to t_____ to in the future?
6 I sometimes l_____ a_____ my grandparents' dog.
7 Please h_____ me to carry these bags into the house.
8 What time does the bus a_____ downtown?

READING

1 Read Marc's blog about technology. Match the best title with blanks 1–3.

a Do we use smartphones differently?
b Do we use different kinds of technology?
c Do we spend different amounts of time online?

2 Read the blog again. Choose the correct words to complete the sentences.

1 The survey says old and young people are _____.
   a the same
   b different
   c both the same and different

2 _____ of older people own an MP3 player.
   a 26%
   b 60%
   c 74%

3 People of different ages all use _____.
   a headphones
   b desktop computers
   c the Internet

4 Marc's grandmother _____ every evening.
   a listens to the radio
   b watches TV
   c goes online

5 Old and young people use their smartphones to _____.
   a take photos
   b make calls
   c watch videos

6 Marc thinks older people play games because _____.
   a they have money
   b they don't work
   c the games are free

REVIEW and PRACTICE 5

HOME BLOG PODCASTS ABOUT CONTACT

Our guest blogger Marc looks at the different ways young and old people use technology.

Technology for the young and old

How old are you? What technology do you have? What do you use it for? How often do you use it? A new survey in the U.S. asks people these questions, and here are some of the results.

1 _____

Can you guess the answer to this question: Which group has more desktop computers: people aged 18–34 or people aged 57–65? The answer is interesting – it's the older group. Can you guess why? It's because young people have laptops and smartphones. They don't need desktop computers! Another interesting result of the survey is about music. Only 26% of people aged 60 and above have an MP3 player. For people in their twenties it's 74%. But does this mean old people don't listen to music? Of course not! My parents often listen to music, but they do it at home. And they like the same music, so they never need headphones!

2 _____

The survey says that almost all ages use the Internet. I think that's interesting because some people think that the Internet is only for young people. In fact, only very old people don't go online. But young people do spend more time online than older people. This doesn't surprise me – most of my friends spend hours on the Internet every day. A lot of us need it for our jobs. But I think old people spend a lot of time using other technology. My grandmother is nearly 80. It's true that she never goes online – she doesn't even have a computer! But she loves listening to the radio and she watches TV for hours every evening. She's very fast with the remote control!

3 _____

One fact from the survey is that most older people only use their smartphones for one or two things. But young people make calls, send messages, go online, buy things, listen to music, and watch videos – all on their smartphones. Both age groups use their smartphones to take photos, but the type of photos is different. Young people love to take selfies! Another fact from the survey was about social media. Old people use it to find old friends and chat with their families. Young people use social media to find new friends. But my favorite fact from the survey was this: it says that old people play a lot of free games online! I think I know why this is – they don't have jobs. It's easy to play games when you have a lot of time!

UNIT 6

Places

6A LANGUAGE

GRAMMAR: there is/are

1 ▶6.1 Complete the conversation with the words in the box. Listen and check.

there are some (3)   there's an
are there any   is there a   there are no
is there an   there's no (3)   there aren't

A In this picture, ¹ _there are some_ pencils.
B ² _____ pen.
A ³ _____ book? No ...
B ⁴ But _____ glasses. Reading glasses.
A ⁵ _____ sunglasses.
B But ⁶ _____ umbrella.
A ⁷ _____ wallet.
B ⁸ _____ credit cards?
A Credit cards? No, ⁹ _____ .
B ¹⁰ _____ key? Yes, one.
A ¹¹ _____ camera.
B But ¹² _____ cell phones – two!

2 Read the information about Nuuk, the capital of Greenland. Then complete the text with *there is/there are*, and *a/an*, *some*, *any*, or *no*.

population	17,000	shopping malls	1
airports	1	cafés & restaurants	10+
schools	5+	art galleries	?
big hotels	1	clubs	?
roads out of town	0	boats and ferries	100s!
parks	0		

Nuuk is the capital of Greenland, but it only has 17,000 people. ¹ _There's an_ airport and ² _____ schools. ³ _____ big hotel, but ⁴ _____ roads out of Nuuk and ⁵ _____ parks. ⁶ _____ shopping mall and ⁷ _____ cafés and restaurants. ⁸ _____ art gallery? I don't think so. What about clubs? ⁹ _____ clubs? I'm not sure. But I know that ¹⁰ _____ boats and ferries – lots of them!

VOCABULARY: Places in a town

3 Order the letters to make places in a town.

1 s t o p   f e c i o f   p_____ o_____
2 h a i l s p o t   h_____
3 v i o m e   r t e a h t e   m_____ t_____
4 b u l c   c_____
5 l e p i c o   n a t t o s i p_____ s_____
6 y g c e o r r   r s e o t   g_____ s_____
7 r a n t i   o s t i n a t   t_____ s_____
8 u s e m u m   m_____

4 Complete the sentences with places in a town.

1 buy clothes, computers, sunglasses, books, etc. in a s_____ m_____
2 catch the bus at the b_____ s_____
3 eat in a c_____ or r_____
4 keep your money in a b_____
5 sleep in a h_____
6 catch a plane from the a_____
7 walk your dog in the p_____
8 learn English at a language s_____

PRONUNCIATION: Linking consonants and vowels

5 ▶6.2 Listen and repeat the sentences. Pay attention to how the sounds link together.

1 There‿are some cafés.
2 There's‿a restaurant.
3 Is there‿a shopping mall?
4 Yes, there‿is. There‿are two schools, too.
5 There‿are eight‿stores.
6 There‿is a post‿office.
7 Are there‿any parks?
8 No, there‿aren't.

34

Skills 6B

READING: Reading in detail

1 Read the article. Who thinks the city is a good place to live – Ursula or Lenny? Who thinks the country is a good place to live? Whose opinion do you agree with, Ursula's or Lenny's?

BIG CITY or COUNTRY?

Where is a better place to live? We ask two friends to give their opinions.

Ursula Is life exciting in the city? In my view, traveling an hour to work every day is not exciting. Also, it's not expensive in the country. Small apartments in big cities are expensive.

People say that it's boring here because it's difficult to find things to do. But I like going for walks and learning about animals and birds. There's lots to do in the city, but I don't think theaters and museums are interesting.

Finally, people are friendly in the country. We say "hi" to everyone. Not like in cities!

Lenny The country is a great place to live … if you like to drive! Why live in a place where you need a car because the movie theater is 20 miles away?

Also, there are no good jobs and the only social life is online. In my opinion, cities are interesting for young people because everything you need is right there.

Also, you don't need a car because you can walk or ride a bike. So city life is good for you and the planet.

2 Read the article again. Choose yes (Y) or no (N). Write the word or phrase in the article that gives you the answer. Use the underlined key words to help you.

1 Does Ursula <u>know</u> Lenny? (Y) / N _friends_
2 Does Ursula think life is <u>exciting in the city</u>? Y / N _____
3 Are there <u>many things to do in the city</u>, in Ursula's opinion? Y / N _____
4 In Ursula's opinion, are <u>cities unfriendly</u>? Y / N _____
5 Does Lenny say cars <u>are necessary in the country</u>? Y / N _____
6 Does Lenny think the <u>country is good for young people</u>? Y / N _____
7 Does Lenny like to have <u>movie theaters, grocery stores, etc. near him</u>? Y / N _____

3 Match the two parts of the sentences.

1 Ursula doesn't like ____   a cities are boring.
2 She doesn't think that the ____   b good places to live.
3 She likes ____   c going for walks.
4 Lenny doesn't think ____   d interesting things to do in cities.
5 He thinks there are ____   e long trips to work.
6 In his view, cities are ____   f country is boring.

4 Complete the parts of the body.

1 It's easy to see where something is with two e___ ___ ___ on the front of our f___ ___ ___.
2 Our e___ ___ ___ are on the side of our h___ ___ ___.
3 There are 32 t___ ___ ___ in an adult's m___ ___ ___ ___, but only 20 in a child's.
4 Your h___ ___ ___ ___ and f___ ___ ___ are at the end of your arms and legs.
5 Our h___ ___ ___ helps to keep us warm!
6 We use our n___ ___ ___ to smell things like food.
7 You can look after your b___ ___ ___ by eating healthy food and exercising.
8 Running long distances can be bad for your k___ ___ ___ ___.

6C LANGUAGE

GRAMMAR: Prepositions of place

1 Choose the correct prepositions to complete the sentences.

1 My pen is _____ your chair. Can you give it to me?
   a between   b in   c under
2 The children's bedroom is very small, so they have "bunk beds" – one bed is _____ the other.
   a above   b next to   c behind
3 I think that new lamp looks good _____ the computer and the window.
   a on   b under   c between
4 We have a bed, a chair, and a table _____ our bedroom.
   a in   b above   c next to
5 Why is the television _____ the desk? We can't watch a movie like that!
   a in front of   b between   c behind
6 There's a beautiful park _____ our apartment. You can see it from our living room.
   a above   b in front of   c in
7 Please put the salad _____ the table for our lunch.
   a on   b under   c next to
8 The train station is _____ the stores. Go through the shopping mall and you can see it on the other side.
   a under   b behind   c above

2 Complete the sentences with the correct prepositions.

1 Come and sit _____ to me. We can do our homework together.
2 Please don't stand in _____ of the refrigerator. I need the milk and some eggs.
3 I can't see my car – it's _____ the house. But I'm sure it's there!
4 He keeps his keys _____ his wallet so he doesn't lose them.
5 It's raining. Do you want to stand _____ my umbrella with me?
6 Is the club _____ the movie theater and the bank?
7 Planes fly _____ our town all day. It's very noisy sometimes!
8 Don't put your dirty feet _____ the table!

VOCABULARY: Rooms and furniture

3 Look at the words in the box. Order the letters then write the words in the correct rooms.

| ~~deb~~ | fosa | vetso | herows |
| bhabtut | ittelo | lcteso | |

bedroom	bathroom
bed	
kitchen	**living room**

4 Look at the picture. Complete the description.

This is my ¹_____. I do my homework here. I have my laptop on this ²_____. There's a large ³_____ above it, so I have lots of light in the day. But in the evening, I turn on my ⁴_____ next to the computer. I have lots of books, so there are some long ⁵_____ between the desk and the ⁶_____ with my coffee cup. My ⁷_____ is big but old, so I sometimes sit on the sofa to study. But my favorite thing? I have a small ⁸_____ under my desk with cold drinks and chocolate. It's my mini-kitchen!

PRONUNCIATION: Sentence stress

5 ▶6.3 Underline the stressed words. Listen and check.

1 My desk is under the window.
2 The table is next to the shelves.
3 Their bathroom is above the kitchen.
4 The chair is between the bed and the closet.
5 His keys are on the chair.
6 Our sofa is in the living room.

SKILLS 6D

SPEAKING: Asking for and giving directions

1 ▶ 6.4 Listen to three conversations. Where do the people want to go?

1 The woman wants to go to the _____.
2 The man wants to go to the _____.
3 The man wants to go to the _____.

2 ▶ 6.4 Listen again and complete the conversations.

Conversation 1

1 _____ me, _____ the park, please?

2 Go _____ this street and turn _____ at the hospital.

Conversation 2

3 Is _____ a police station around _____?

4 _____ right just before the post office. You can see it _____ the post office, on the _____.

Conversation 3

5 Is the museum _____ here?

6 Go down _____ street for about three or four _____ and then turn right _____ the shopping mall.

3 ▶ 6.5 Listen to the conversation. Which place does the man call?

a the post office
b the movie theater
c the swimming pool

4 ▶ 6.6 Listen again to six extracts from the conversation in exercise 3. Match each extract with the ways of checking information (a–c).

1 ____
2 ____
3 ____
4 ____
5 ____
6 ____

a asking someone to repeat
b asking someone to speak more slowly
c asking a question to check the information

37

6 REVIEW and PRACTICE

HOME BLOG **PODCASTS** ABOUT CONTACT

Tom and Sam talk about Brad's house.

LISTENING

1 ▶ 6.7 Listen to the podcast about a very small house. Check (✓) the things Brad has in his house.

a stove _____
b table _____
c sofa _____
d chair _____
e desk _____
f bathtub _____
g shower _____
h toilet _____
i closet _____
j bed _____

2 ▶ 6.7 Listen again. Write T (true), F (false), or NG (not given) if there is no information in the podcast.

1 Tom says that Sam has lots of parties. _____
2 There are thirteen small houses near Brad. _____
3 Brad has a large yard at the front of his house. _____
4 Brad cooks every day. _____
5 There are four chairs in the living room. _____
6 Brad's friends visit him on Saturdays. _____
7 Brad prefers showers to baths. _____
8 Brad's bed is in the closet. _____
9 Brad pays $600 each month for his house. _____
10 Brad wants to live in a different house when he is older. _____

READING

1 Read Penny's blog about New York. Choose the correct sentence.

a The three places are all free.
b You can see art at all these places.
c All the places are very old.

2 Read the blog again. Match the sentences with places a–c.

1 Some visitors don't know it's there. _____
2 This place is new and also free. _____
3 There are good places to eat here. _____
4 You can see movies here. _____
5 It's easy to go there by bus. _____
6 There are beautiful views when you walk here. _____

a the High Line   b the Cloisters
c Williamsburg

3 Complete the sentences with places in a town.

1 Is there a p _ _ _ o _ _ _ _ e near here? I need to buy some stamps.
2 Daisy broke her leg and had to go to the h _ _ _ _ _ _ l.
3 Let's go to a c _ _ _ this evening and go dancing!
4 Can you go to the g _ _ _ _ _ y s _ _ _ _ and buy some bread and milk, please?
5 Shall we get our tickets online or from the t _ _ _ _ s _ _ _ _ _ n?
6 We stayed at a really expensive h _ _ _ l when we visited Barcelona.
7 I usually buy presents at the s _ _ _ _ _ _ g m _ _ _ in town.
8 Nick left his wallet on the bus and had to go to the p _ _ _ _ e s _ _ _ _ _ n.
9 Which s _ _ _ _ l do his children go to?
10 I spent all my money, so I went to the b _ _ k to get some more.

REVIEW and PRACTICE 6

HOME BLOG PODCASTS ABOUT CONTACT

This week's guest blogger Penny writes about the New York hosts' favorite places.

Enjoying the "Big Apple"

At the New York studio, we're really lucky to live in a fantastic city with lots to see and do. There are many parks and museums and there are so many restaurants and cafés. It's not easy to choose, but I want to tell you about our favorite places in the city.

Penny

My favorite place is the High Line, a new park in Midtown Manhattan. Before, it was a train line, but now it is a park above the city, about a mile long. I love walking, and this is a great place to walk. And there are amazing views of the city and the Hudson River. There are also many plants and flowers to look at on the way, and some very good street art, all free. There are lots of different entrances but the easiest for me is between 11th and 12th Avenues on 34th Street. I often go on the weekend, when I have time.

I love a museum called the Cloisters, in northern Manhattan. Not many tourists know about it, and it is pretty far from downtown. But it's easy to travel there because there is a bus stop next to it. It's about $25 to get in, so I don't go very often. But it's fantastic! At the center is a really old building and there's lots of interesting old art to see. And there are some beautiful gardens in front of the castle. I like going there because it's very quiet.

Ethan

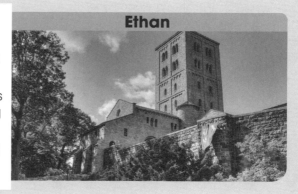

Marc

On the weekend, I sometimes go to Williamsburg in Brooklyn. It's an exciting part of the city, where you can go to fantastic cafés or just walk around the markets and enjoy the atmosphere. I love looking at the street art. There is also a great movie theater on Grand Street. There are seven screens and seats for nearly 1,000 people! People from all over the world live in Williamsburg, and everyone is really friendly. If you want to go shopping, it's great for fresh food and old clothes.

These are our favorite places, but what about you? Tell us about your favorite places in your city!

UNIT 7 All in the past

7A LANGUAGE

GRAMMAR: Simple past: be

1 Complete the sentences with *was*, *were*, *wasn't*, or *weren't*.

1 Where _____ you on Tuesday?
2 Oh, good. You have your cell phone. Where _____ it?
3 The movie _____ very good. Don't go and see it.
4 My grandmother _____ a doctor when most doctors _____ men.
5 The children _____ very noisy yesterday. I hope they're quiet today.
6 The windows are open now, but they _____ this morning.
7 We _____ in bed until after 2 a.m. I'm really tired today!
8 My hair _____ brown when I _____ a baby. It's black now.
9 "_____ Lucy at the party?" "Yes, she _____."
10 "_____ you bored in the hospital?" "No, I _____. I read some good books."

2 Rewrite the sentences and questions in the simple past.

1 I am a taxi driver.
   I was a taxi driver.
2 He's not with us. He's at the shopping mall.
   _____
3 Those students aren't very friendly. They are unfriendly.
   _____
4 She's not at home. She's at the park.
   _____
5 "Are the pizzas cheap?" "Yes, they are."
   _____
6 "I'm not very happy." "I am!"
   _____
7 "Are your exams difficult?' "No, they're not."
   _____
8 "Is she your teacher?" "No, she's not."
   _____
9 Sam's not in class this week. He's on vacation.
   _____
10 "Is this question difficult to understand?" "No, it's not."
   _____

VOCABULARY: Celebrities

3 Match the celebrity words with a or b.

1 artist _____
2 athlete _____
3 DJ _____
4 movie director _____
5 soccer player _____
6 musician _____
7 racing driver _____
8 writer _____

a arts and entertainment
b sports

4 Complete the words for celebrities.

1 Most f___ ___ ___ ___ ___ m___ ___ ___ ___ are young and beautiful.
2 P___ ___ ___ ___ ___ ___ ___ ___ ___ ___ are public people, but they're not celebrities. They help people but aren't always famous.
3 He works for *The Daily Planet* newspaper and is an excellent j___ ___ ___ ___ ___ ___ ___ ___.
4 Were the K___ ___ ___ and Q___ ___ ___ ___ of Spain in London last week?
5 I love my work as a ballet d___ ___ ___ ___ ___, but the shows are difficult!
6 Now we can all be good p___ ___ ___ ___ ___ ___ ___ ___ ___ ___ with a digital camera.
7 She wants to be a famous t___ ___ ___ ___ p___ ___ ___ ___ ___ and win Wimbledon one day!
8 Do you find paintings by the Mexican a___ ___ ___ ___ ___ Diego Rivera interesting?

PRONUNCIATION: *was/were*

5 ▶ 7.1 Listen and repeat the questions and answers. Pay attention to the pronunciation of *was* and *were*.

1 A Where was he yesterday?
  B He was at home.
2 A Where were you on Friday?
  B I was at the post office.
3 A Where were they last week?
  B They were in Turkey.
4 A Where was your sister in June?
  B She was with my grandparents.
5 A Where was I on Saturday night?
  B You were at the club.
6 A Where were your parents in 1980?
  B They were in college.

SKILLS 7B

LISTENING: Listening for dates

1 ▶ 7.2 Listen to the information. Match the celebrities with three of the words in the box.

| actor | dancer | king | musician | politician |
| queen | sports player | travel writer | | |

1 Ira Aldridge _____
2 Kumar Shri Ranjitsinhji _____
3 Isabella Bird _____

2 ▶ 7.2 Listen again. Complete the information about each person.

1 These three celebrities were famous in the _____ century.
2 Aldridge was in the UK from _____ until _____.
3 He was alive from July 24, 1807 until _____ _____.
4 Ranjitsinhji played for an English university team in the year _____.
5 His first national game for England was on _____ _____ _____.
6 Bird was _____ years old when she started traveling.
7 Her first book was in _____.
8 She was _____ years old when she was in Morocco.

3 ▶ 7.3 Listen and complete the sentences.

1 _____ _____ athlete.
2 The _____ is called "_____ _____."
3 Before she _____ _____ artist, she _____ _____ clerk.
4 My _____ _____ _____ _____ on Fridays and Saturdays.
5 He was born on _____ _____ -first, 1987.
6 The last time I _____ _____ a concert was _____ _____ in May.

4 Write the correct dates.

1 3/4 is ~~May~~ fourth.   _March_
2 8/15 is August fifth.   _____
3 4/10 is April second.   _____
4 1/2 is January twelfth.   _____
5 10/30 is November thirtieth.   _____
6 7/21 is June twenty-first.   _____
7 2/6 is February fifth.   _____
8 9/9 is September nineteenth.   _____

41

7C LANGUAGE

GRAMMAR: Simple past: regular verbs

1 Order the words to make questions.

1 live / you / in the 2000s / did / where
   _____?
2 did / listen to / music / you / then
   _____?
3 was / your / favorite / singer / who
   _____?
4 they / did / sing / what
   _____?
5 an instrument / did / play / you
   _____?
6 the name of / what / your band / was
   _____?

2 Complete the sentences and questions. Use the verbs in parentheses in the simple past.

1 In South America, we _____ (visit) Colombia, Brazil and Peru.
2 "_____ (you/travel) to Berlin last year?" "Yes, I _____."
3 I _____ (not/watch) the game. Was it good?
4 She _____ (study) all day and all night before her final exam.
5 "_____ (he/arrive) at work on time this morning?" "No, _____. He was late again!"
6 After school they _____ (listen) to music.
7 We _____ (cook) chicken and vegetables for dinner yesterday.
8 "_____ (she/use) the remote control this morning?" "Yes, _____."
9 We _____ (not/like) the furniture in our hotel room.
10 The train trip was very long! The train _____ (stop) at lots of stations.

VOCABULARY: Time expressions

3 Which word does not make a time expression with the underlined word?

1 <u>last</u> month / morning / night / year
2 <u>on</u> six o'clock / February 10 / the weekend / April 18
3 <u>in</u> 1997 / the last decade / last year / the sixties
4 <u>on</u> 2004 / Wednesday / July 16 / Saturday
5 two fifteen / days / weeks / years <u>ago</u>
6 <u>yesterday</u> morning / afternoon / evening / night
7 on / last / in / this <u>Monday</u>
8 three weeks / a year / an hour / Wednesday <u>ago</u>

4 Complete the sentences with time expressions.

1 We worked until 2:00 a.m. last _____. We're very tired this morning!
2 When did I lose my passport? About 24 hours ago, so _____ afternoon.
3 She got her first job _____ 2012, and she works for the same company today.
4 Where was your summer vacation _____ year?
5 His computer stopped working _____ two o'clock this afternoon.
6 I met my girlfriend three months _____ at the bus stop!
7 They bought the GPS _____ Tuesday and now it doesn't work.
8 Did your mother and father meet in _____ 1980s?
9 My birthday is _____ January 24.
10 Did they go bike riding _____ the weekend?

PRONUNCIATION: -ed endings

5 ▶ 7.4 Complete each story 1–3 with three sentences a–i. For each story, choose only sentences where the -ed endings of the verbs in bold are pronounced the same (/d/, /t/, or /ɪd/). Then listen, check, and repeat.

1 Debbie **loved** trains when she was a student.
   _b_ ___ ___
2 Edwina **needed** to go to the shopping mall.
   ___ ___ ___
3 Tina **watched** a movie in the afternoon.
   ___ ___ ___

a Then, in the evening, she **cooked** dinner.
b In 2017, she **traveled** to Boston.
c She **wanted** to buy a present for her boyfriend.
d She **tried** to win, but her friend was very good.
e But she was sad, so she **walked** to a club.
f She met a friend there and they **played** tennis.
g But everything was expensive and it **started** to rain.
h She **danced** all night there with her friends.
i She **visited** her brother, instead.

SKILLS 7D

WRITING: Writing informal e-mails

1 Read the e-mail. Then number the sentences 1–5.

Hi Geeta,

How are you? I hope the family is all well.

I'm in the UK! I wanted to tell you about my trip to Ramsgate with my friends from class on Saturday. It was fantastic! We started early and traveled by train. We arrived at ten o'clock. First, we visited a museum and listened to an interesting tour guide talk about the history of Ramsgate. Then we ate fish and chips in an old pub. After that, we walked around Ramsgate, but we were tired, so we stopped on the beach and had ice cream. It was a traditional day at the English seaside!

Please tell me your news. Did you do anything special on the weekend?

Take care,

Mishiko

a They sat next to the ocean. ____
b They arrived in Ramsgate. ____
c They learned about the town's past. ____
d They looked at the town. ____
e They had lunch. ____

2 Choose the correct options to complete 1–7.

1_____ James,
How are 2_____?
I hope 3_____ are well.
Did I 4_____ you about my vacation? We went to Marrakech in Morocco. It's an amazing place! Here's a photo of me in the local market.
Take 5_____ and 6_____ you soon!
Bye for 7_____,
Tracey

1	a Bye	b See	c Hi
2	a well	b things	c they
3	a things	b you	c it
4	a tell	b ask	c want
5	a soon	b care	c well
6	a see	b are	c hope
7	a well	b you	c now

3 Number the pictures 1–3. Then complete the sentences with the verbs in parentheses.

1 Nora arrived home at seven thirty.
First, _____ (listen).
Then _____ (cook).
After that, _____ (work) in her office.

2 Gavin had a very busy day.
First, _____ (help) his mom.
Then _____ (play) soccer.
After that, _____ (visit) his aunt.

4 Reply to Mishiko's e-mail. Tell her what you did last weekend. Make sure you:

- start and end your e-mail in a friendly way.
- use sequencers to show the order of events.

7 REVIEW and PRACTICE

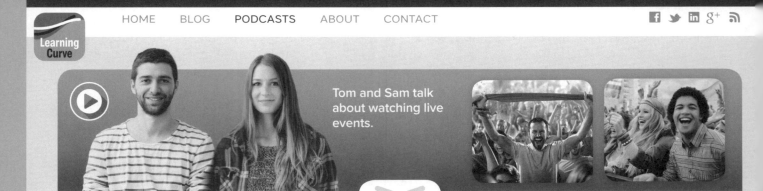

HOME   BLOG   PODCASTS   ABOUT   CONTACT

LISTENING

1 ▶ 7.5 Listen to the podcast about live events. Check (✓) the correct box for each person.

	Live	TV
Speaker 1 prefers		
Speaker 2 prefers		
Speaker 3 prefers		
Speaker 4 prefers		
Tom prefers		
Sam prefers		

2 ▶ 7.5 Listen again. Complete the sentences with one word from the podcast.

1 The survey said that _____ people prefer live events to TV.
2 Speaker 1 _____ watches soccer on TV.
3 He likes singing songs with his _____.
4 The weather at the _____ festival wasn't good.
5 Speaker 2 and her friends danced for _____.
6 Speaker 3 says the _____ was boring.
7 She can see the _____ better on TV.
8 Speaker 4 likes looking at _____ in art galleries.
9 He went to a gallery a few _____ ago.
10 Sam says that Tom is _____ because he prefers TV to live events.

READING

1 Read Simon's blog about celebrities. Match the celebrities with their jobs in photos a–d.

1 Hugh Jackman _____
2 Lady Gaga _____
3 Kanye West _____
4 Jennifer Hudson _____

2 Read the blog again. Write T (true), F (false), or NG (not given) if there is no information in the blog.

1 Hugh Jackman was in eight *X-Men* movies. _____
2 He lived in England for twelve months. _____
3 Lady Gaga helps other people. _____
4 She worked as a waitress to pay for school. _____
5 Kanye West didn't like working in the store. _____
6 His parents paid for all his clothes. _____
7 His company's clothes are expensive. _____
8 *Dreamgirls* is a movie about a restaurant. _____
9 Jennifer Hudson was born in Chicago. _____
10 She pays for her burgers at Burger King. _____

3 Order the letters to make celebrity jobs.

1 i v e o m   t i r e d r o c   m_____ d_____
2 c a r n i g   r i d r e v   r_____ d_____
3 o c s e c r   y p a e r l   s_____ p_____
4 h e a l t e t   a_____
5 n o i s h a f   d o l e m   f_____ m_____
6 n e t s i n   r e y a l p   t_____ p_____
7 t e r r i w   w_____
8 s m i n c i u a   m_____

REVIEW and PRACTICE 7

HOME BLOG PODCASTS ABOUT CONTACT

Our guest blogger Simon tells us what some stars of music and movies did in the past.

Before they were STARS

Most celebrities spend their days doing really cool and exciting things. But their lives weren't always so interesting. In fact, some celebrities had very normal jobs before they were famous.

In 2000, **Hugh Jackman** played the part of Wolverine in *X-Men*. The movie was very successful, and he was the star of eight more X-Movies in the 2000s and the 2010s. But Hugh had other jobs before he was an actor. When he was only eighteen he moved to England from Australia. He was a teacher in a very expensive school. His students liked him very much, but after a year he moved back to Australia.

These days everyone knows **Lady Gaga** for her music, her amazing shows, and her interesting clothes. She sells millions of records and she works for a lot of charities. On December 11, 2015, people chose her as the "Woman of the Year, 2015". But before she was famous, when she was in school, she worked as a waitress near her home in New York. She says she wanted the money to buy an expensive purse!

When **Kanye West** was a teenager, he worked in a clothing store. He liked the clothes, but he didn't enjoy the job. And he didn't make much money. In fact, he didn't earn enough money to buy the clothes in the store! Today he is one of the most famous musicians in the world and makes millions and millions of dollars. In 2015, his company started selling clothes. And they're not cheap!

Jennifer Hudson is a very famous actress and singer. She was the star of the movie *Dreamgirls* in 2006. But her first job was at a Burger King restaurant in Chicago. She started work in the restaurant when she was sixteen. Everyone says she liked to sing a lot at work! In 2007, Burger King called Jennifer to say she never needs to pay for food – she gets free food for life!

Travel

GRAMMAR: Simple past: irregular verbs

1 Write the simple past verbs.

1. We h_____ a loud noise from the street.
2. Karen s_____ her money on clothes.
3. No one k_____ the answer to her question.
4. Who t_____ you English last year?
5. Brendan f_____ a wallet on the bus.
6. Sue w_____ a letter to her grandmother.
7. They b_____ some vegetables at the market.
8. He c_____ a new lamp for his office.

2 Complete the sentences with the simple past verbs.

Across

1. This shirt only _____ me $20 at the shopping mall.
3. She _____ her house keys in her purse.
5. I _____ my boyfriend in college in 2016.
6. They _____ to Cartagena in an old car.
7. He _____ me a book to read.
8. It _____ three days to paint our new house.

Down

1. I _____ to work early yesterday.
2. Her cat _____ next to her on the sofa.
4. Hi! I _____ you were on vacation this week – why are you at work?
6. We _____ housework, and then went to bed early.

VOCABULARY: Travel verbs

3 Choose one option in each sentence which is not correct.

1. He *got in / got on / took* a taxi to the station.
2. Do you know how to ride a *bike / horse / car*?
3. I don't want to miss my *bike / bus / train* tomorrow!
4. Let's take *a taxi / a bus / a car* to the hospital.
5. They *flew / got off / sailed* from Panamá to Colombia.
6. We can book our *flight / hotel / subway* on the Internet.
7. Where do we *walk / get off / take* the train?
8. They *got off / got on / got lost* the bus at the grocery store.

4 Complete the sentences with travel verbs.

1. _____ the car, please. We need to leave now!
2. Can I _____ the flight online now, or do I need my passport?
3. I _____ the train to work. It gives me time to read and relax.
4. If you _____ the bus you need to wait for the next one.
5. Is it OK if we _____ to the park? It's a lovely evening and I don't have a bike.
6. You don't want to _____, so take a good map.
7. Most people prefer to _____ long distances because planes are fast.
8. She can't _____ her motorcycle to work this week because her brother has it.
9. The ferry doesn't _____ when there is bad weather.
10. To go to the museum, take the subway and _____ at the third station.

PRONUNCIATION: Irregular simple past verbs

5 ▶ 8.1 Choose the correct sound for the verbs in each sentence. Then listen, check, and repeat.

1 Bob got on the train at 6 a.m.	/ɑ/	/ɔ/	/ow/
2 Do you know he rode home?	/ɑ/	/ɔ/	/ow/
3 He walked to town and saw his friends.	/ɑ/	/ɔ/	/ow/
4 I thought I saw a tour guide.	/ɑ/	/ɔ/	/ow/
5 She drove to Rome.	/ɑ/	/ɔ/	/ow/
6 Paul lost his ticket.	/ɑ/	/ɔ/	/ow/
7 They chose a cheap hotel.	/ɑ/	/ɔ/	/ow/

SKILLS 8B

READING: Understanding the main idea

1 Write the words for weather and seasons.

1. It's w_____ and cl_____ today.
2. It's s_____ in Canada.
3. In Chicago, it's r_____ now.
4. In the mornings, it's often f_____, but by lunchtime, it's nearly always s_____.
5. F_____ and s_____ are good seasons to visit southern Europe.
6. When it's s_____ in North America, it's w_____ in South America.

2 Look at the title and the photos. Read the first sentences of each paragraph. Which question does the article answer?

a. Why do we travel to places with warm weather?
b. Why do people go to places with bad weather?
c. Which countries have hot, cold, and windy weather?

3 Read the whole article and choose the correct options.

1. The Marathon des Sables runners do the event in
   a. hot weather b. cold weather c. hot and cold weather.
2. Mauro Prosperi got lost because
   a. it was very hot b. the weather was bad
   c. he didn't have any water.
3. Scott's team went to Cape Crozier because
   a. they wanted to be the first people there.
   b. their friends were there.
   c. they wanted to find something.
4. During the Antarctic trip, the men didn't see
   a. the sun. b. many penguins. c. any other people.
5. Windsurfers at the Défi races
   a. come from many different countries.
   b. sometimes travel at 144 kilometers an hour.
   c. are all French.
6. The windsurfing speed record was in
   a. France. b. Namibia. c. Gruissan.

4 Complete the sentences with the correct option.

1. It is *not very / pretty* foggy today – I can see the top of those hills.
2. Don't drink that coffee! It's *not very / really* hot! Wait a few minutes.
3. I don't want to read the rest of this book. It's *not very / pretty* good.
4. I'm *not very / really* surprised you are here. I thought you were in Brazil.
5. It was *not very / pretty* cold this morning. I needed a sweater when I wasn't in the sun.
6. That wasn't a good horror movie last night. I was *pretty / not very* scared at all!
7. Our exam was *pretty / really* easy. Some questions were difficult, but I'm sure I passed.
8. You got three pizzas for only $12? That's *not very / really* cheap!

Usually, when we travel, we go to places where the weather is warm and sunny. We don't like it when it's very hot, cold, windy, or foggy. But some people look for extreme weather. Are they crazy? You decide!

A **The Marathon des Sables is a six-day, 200-kilometer trek through the Sahara desert in southern Morocco.** Runners carry everything they need with them, including water. It can reach 50°C, but at night, they often sleep in temperatures below 0°! In 1994, Italian athlete Mauro Prosperi got lost for nine days after a sand storm. He ran 299 kilometers in the wrong direction … into Algeria!

B **In July 1911, three members of Scott's team to the Antarctic traveled to a place called Cape Crozier.** The men walked for 19 days in the 24-hour darkness of the Antarctic winter. They carried their food and tent behind them. It was sometimes –70°C. Why? They went to collect penguin eggs!

C **Every year, more than a thousand windsurfers from 40 countries go to Gruissan in southern France for the Défi Wind races.** This is an excellent place for windsurfing because it's very windy, with winds sometimes reaching 144 kilometers an hour. But Antoine Albeau holds the windsurfing speed record. He was in Namibia when he traveled at 98 kilometers an hour on November 2nd, 2015.

8C LANGUAGE

GRAMMAR: *there was/were*

1 Match the two parts of the sentences.

1 At the party, there was some ____
2 There was a ____
3 There was ____
4 There were ____
5 There were lots ____
6 There weren't ____
7 Was there ____
8 Were there ____

a a photographer? Yes, there was!
b no singer.
c any celebrities? No, there weren't.
d any waiters or waitresses.
e DJ all evening.
f of friendly people.
g great music.
h some sandwiches and cakes.

2 Complete the dialogue with *there was/were* in the correct form.

Pablo	Grandfather, ¹_____ any stores here in 1950?
Grandfather	Oh, yes, ²_____ lots of stores, but ³_____ only one shopping mall, and it was small.
Pablo	And what about places to eat?
Grandfather	Well, ⁴_____ some cafés, but ⁵_____ any pizza restaurants or places like that.
Pablo	⁶_____ a swimming pool?
Grandfather	No, ⁷_____. But ⁸_____ a park if you wanted to go for a walk.
Pablo	And what about transportation? ⁹_____ a train station?
Grandfather	Yes, ¹⁰_____. It was very important, because ¹¹_____ many cars in those days.
Pablo	And what did you do in the evenings?
Grandfather	Well, ¹²_____ no club for young people like there is today.
Pablo	That sounds boring!

VOCABULARY: Nature

3 ▶8.2 Complete each sentence with the words in the box. Then decide which picture each sentence describes. Listen and check.

| grass | river | ocean | sky | sun | trees |

1 You can see it's windy today. Look at the _____!   a b
2 There are some beautiful _____ above the water.   a b
3 The evening _____ is very clear today.   a b
4 The _____ next to the water looks very soft.   a b
5 I don't think the water goes very fast along this _____.   a b
6 You can still see the _____, but not for much longer.   a b

4 Complete the nature words.

1 I can see a large black c___ ___ ___ ___ in the sky.
2 My dog loves to play in the f___ ___ ___ ___ next to our apartment.
3 Those f___ ___ ___ ___ ___ ___ are all different colors: red, yellow, and pink.
4 It's summer, but it's not hot up here on the m___ ___ ___ ___ ___ ___ ___.
5 We had lunch on the b___ ___ ___ ___, but it was pretty hot.
6 There are more than twenty types of trees in this f___ ___ ___ ___ ___ ___.

PRONUNCIATION: Sentence stress

5 ▶8.3 Underline the stressed words. Then listen, check, and repeat.

1 "Was there a television in your room?" "No, there wasn't."
2 "Was there an evening meal?" "Yes, there was."
3 "Were there any clubs?" "Yes, there were."
4 "Were there good restaurants?" "No, there weren't."
5 "Was there any music?" "Yes, there was."
6 "Were there many nice people?" "No, there weren't!"
7 "Were there any stores?" "Yes, there were."
8 "Was there a swimming pool?" "No, there wasn't."

SKILLS 8D

SPEAKING: Buying a ticket

1 ▶ 8.4 Listen to two telephone conversations. Find one mistake in A and one mistake in B and write the correct information.

1 Conversation 1: _____
2 Conversation 2: _____

A

B

2 ▶ 8.4 Listen again. Number the phrases 1–8 in the order you hear them.

a I'd like a ticket to Glasgow, please. _____
b When do you want to travel? _____
c Would you like a one-way or round-trip ticket? _____
d What time does the flight leave? _____
e How much is it? _____
f I'd like a one-way ticket to Brazil, please. _____
g When does it arrive? _____
h What kind of ticket would you like? _____

3 ▶ 8.5 Order the words to make sentences and questions. Then listen and check.

1 a / Brisbane / I'd / like / round-trip / ticket / to
_____.

2 does / it / time / leave / what
_____?

3 arrive / does / in / London / it / when
_____?

4 a / like / you / one-way / or / round-trip / ticket / would
_____?

5 $8.90 / a / for / it's / one-way / ticket
_____.

6 do / return / to / want / when / you
_____?

4 ▶ 8.6 Listen and complete the conversations.

1 A _____, FPQ Couriers. _____ _____ Hanif speaking. How can I help you?
B Good _____. I'd like to speak to Mr. Travers, please.
A Who's calling?
B _____ _____ _____ Diane Godridge.
~
C Thanks for _____, Ms. Godridge. Goodbye.
B _____.

2 A Good _____. Jessica _____.
B Hello. _____ _____ William Sharp from Oldham Print Services. Is Karen there, please?
~
C Thanks for _____ _____, William.
B Thank you, Karen. _____ for now.

8 REVIEW and PRACTICE

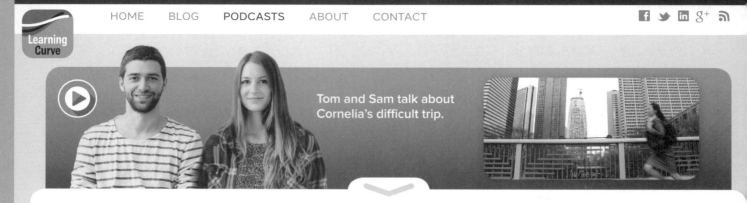

HOME   BLOG   PODCASTS   ABOUT   CONTACT

Tom and Sam talk about Cornelia's difficult trip.

LISTENING

1 ▶ 8.7 Listen to the podcast about a bad trip. Number the things that happened (a–h) in the correct order (1–8).

- a Cornelia took a taxi. _____
- b She asked a woman for help. _____
- c She used the Internet. _____
- d She went to a café. _____
- e She ran very fast. _____
- f She got an e-mail. _____
- g She fell over. _____
- h She asked a man for help. _____

2 ▶ 8.7 Listen again. Choose the correct answers.

1. Cornelia got _____ about the interview.
   a a letter   b an e-mail   c a phone call
2. Cornelia's interview was _____ miles from her home.
   a 300   b 200   c 100
3. She didn't fly because there weren't any _____ flights.
   a early   b cheap   c quick
4. She didn't know the _____ of her interview.
   a time   b address   c date
5. She took a _____ home from the station.
   a bus   b train   c taxi
6. The train was very _____.
   a fast   b expensive   c slow
7. At the station, she asked a _____ for directions.
   a man   b woman   c tourist
8. There were only _____ minutes before the interview.
   a five   b fifteen   c 50
9. Cornelia had her interview in _____.
   a an office   b a store   c a café
10. Cornelia didn't get _____.
    a the job   b a coffee   c an interview

READING

1 Read Marc's blog about South Korea. Match paragraphs 1–4 with photos a–d.

1 _____
2 _____
3 _____
4 _____

2 Read the blog again. Write Y (yes), N (no), or DS (doesn't say) if there is no information in the blog.

1. Marc thinks Korea is horrible in the summer. _____
2. A lot of people go to Imjado beach. _____
3. The weather in the fall is always warm. _____
4. Marc thinks fall is the best time to visit Seoul forest. _____
5. It snows all over South Korea. _____
6. There are many mountains in Korea. _____
7. You can't ski near Seoul. _____
8. Spring is everyone's favorite season in South Korea. _____
9. Marc doesn't like cherry blossoms. _____
10. Koreans often travel along the river by bike. _____

REVIEW and PRACTICE 8

HOME   BLOG   PODCASTS   ABOUT   CONTACT

This week's guest blogger Marc tells us why his parents' home country is a great place to visit at all times of the year.

SOUTH KOREA
a country for all seasons!

1 Summer (June to August)

When I was young, people always said to me, "Don't come to Korea in summer – it's horrible!" It's true that it is very hot, but this is a good reason to go to the beach! The most famous beach is Haeundae near the city of Busan. It is very popular in the summer, with thousands of people enjoying the sun. In fact, sometimes it's not very nice because of all the people. So try the island of Imjado for its quiet beach and beautiful ocean.

2 Fall (September to November)

The weather in the fall starts pretty warm, but by the end of the season it's cold. If you are in the capital city, I recommend a visit to the Seoul Forest. It's a very big park downtown with more than 400,000 trees. Fall is the perfect time to visit because the leaves on the trees are all different colors. It's beautiful!

3 Winter (December to February)

South Korea in winter is very cold and windy, and it snows a lot in the north of the country, but there are still fun things to do. Remember that it has a lot of mountains, so it's easy to find a place to ski. The best places to ski are in the east of the country, but that's not the only place. You can even go on a skiing day-trip from Seoul. Then go to a concert or music festival in the evening. There is a lot of live music in Seoul.

4 Spring (March to May)

After the cold (and sometimes difficult) winter, people are always happy at the start of spring. It often seems like everybody is out looking at the new flowers! South Korea is famous for its cherry blossoms – I think they are the most beautiful flowers in the world! When they're not looking at flowers, people often spend spring days bike riding along the Han river. It's a long river with large areas of grass on either side. It's a very good way to get some sun on your face!

UNIT 9 Shopping

9A LANGUAGE

GRAMMAR: Present continuous

1 Choose the correct options to complete the sentences.

1 What's Vicky *made / makes / making* in the kitchen right now?
2 Mia and Lucas *are / do / is* helping their brother with his new phone.
3 "Are you reading to Emily?" "Yes, I *am / do / reading*. It's her favorite book."
4 I'm not *use / uses / using* my bike this week.
5 Gloria and I *aren't / don't / 's not* talking to each other these days.
6 *Am / Are / Is* you and your friends getting ready to go out right now?
7 "Are Luka and Ibrahim playing basketball?" "No they *'re not / don't / 's not*. It's handball."
8 Adam *am / 're not / 's not* working in the office today.
9 Rebecca's *watched / watches / watching* soccer with her friends right now.
10 "Are we going to the grocery store?" "Yes, we *am / are / go*."

2 Complete the sentences with the correct form of the verbs in parentheses.

1 A What _____ right now? (do)
   B I'm on the bus. _____ to school. (go)
2 A _____ at a hotel this week? (stay)
   B No, we _____. We're in our tent. It's cold!
3 A I can hear another person with you. Who _____ to? (talk)
   B That's my grandmother. _____ her today. (visit)
4 A _____ in the competition? (sing)
   B Yes, they _____. They're on stage right now.
5 A _____ Dad _____ lunch ready? (get)
   B No, he _____ cookies. I love his cooking! (make)
6 A What _____ in the bathroom? (do)
   B She _____ a shower. (take)
7 A _____ to California today? (drive)
   B Yes, but we _____ at a restaurant now. The driver needs to take a break. (stop)
8 A _____ anyone _____ here right now? (sit)
   B No, that seat's free. And I _____ now, so you can have both seats! (leave)

VOCABULARY: Clothes

3 Complete the clothes words.

1 I like these s_____ and s_____ – they look good on my big feet!
2 It's snowing. Put a c_____ and h_____ on.
3 She wore a long red d_____ and a pair of beautiful brown b_____.
4 This s_____ keeps me warm in winter.
5 These p_____ are very big. I need a b_____ to make them stay up.
6 On weekends, I wear my old pair of blue j_____ and T-_____ with my favorite bands on them.

4 Look at the pictures and complete the crossword.

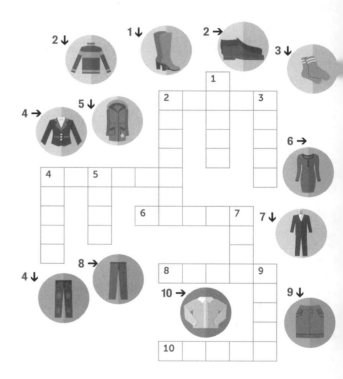

PRONUNCIATION: -ing endings

5 ▶9.1 Listen and repeat. Pay attention to the /ŋ/ sound.

1 Why are you going out?
2 Who's helping me do housework?
3 I'm staying on my own.
4 I think she's speaking in Swahili.
5 We're just arriving now.
6 They're not looking after the house very well.

SKILLS 9B

LISTENING: Identifying key points

1 ▶ 9.2 Listen to the podcast about the meanings of colors. Match the colors with the feelings.

1 in love   ____
2 angry   ____ ____
3 calm   ____ ____ ____
4 sad   ____ ____ ____
5 scared   ____

a black
b blue
c green
d red
e white
f yellow

2 ▶ 9.2 Read these sentences from the podcast. Match them with a or b. Listen again and check.

1 So once again, colors change their meaning in different countries.   ____
2 Red hearts and red flowers show people that you love them.   ____
3 The reason for this is that when we are angry our faces are red.   ____
4 Not just different – totally different!   ____

a emphasizing or repeating
b giving examples or more information

3 ▶ 9.3 Listen to six sentences. Write the filler word (*uh*, *so*, *um*, or *well*) that you hear.

1 _____   4 _____
2 _____   5 _____
3 _____   6 _____

4 Complete the conversations with the correct adjectives.

1 angry / surprised
   A Please don't be _____. I used all your milk. I'm sorry.
   B I'm just a little _____ because you don't drink milk!

2 excited / worried
   A Are you _____ about starting a new school?
   B Yes, I am. I'm happy, but I'm a little _____, too. I hope the other students aren't unfriendly!

3 thirsty / hungry
   A Are you feeling _____? Do you want a sandwich?
   B No, but I am a bit _____. Can I have some juice?

4 calm / scared
   A My sister is _____ by movies like *Dracula* and *Frankenstein*.
   B They certainly don't make me feel _____!

5 happy / tired
   A Your brother doesn't look _____. Is he OK?
   B He's fine, but he's pretty _____. It was a long day at work.

6 bored / sad
   A I'm not _____ that I didn't stay at the party. It was noisy, and the food wasn't good.
   B You did the right thing. I stayed and I was really _____!

9C LANGUAGE

GRAMMAR: *How often* + expressions of frequency

1 Number the frequency expressions 1–10, from the least often to the most often.

a every month _____
b every week _____
c every year _____
d four times a year _____
e never _1_
f once a day _____
g twice a day _____
h twice a week _____
i twice a year _____
j two or three times a month _____

2 Order the words to make sentences and questions.

1 A does / her family / how / Lupita / often / visit
   _____?
   B a / goes / she / twice / usually / year
   _____.

2 A every / exercise / he / week / does
   _____?
   B a / goes / the gym / he / month / once / to
   _____.

3 A a / a / haircut / have / I / twice / year
   _____.
   B not / often / that's / very
   _____!

4 A do / how / their parents / see / often / they
   _____?
   B times / three / month / them / they / a / visit
   _____.

5 A check / day / do / your e-mails / every / you
   _____?
   B a / day / four / I / check / or / three / times / them
   _____.

6 A always / does / go out / on / Saturdays / she
   _____?
   B a / goes / month / once / or / she / out / twice
   _____.

VOCABULARY: Shopping

3 ▶9.4 Number the sentences 1–9 in the correct order to make a paragraph. Then listen and check.

a I usually shop at the market. It's friendly, but you have to pay with … _1_
b … credit card at the shopping … _____
c … cash there. You can pay by … _____
d … mall. For presents, I sometimes go to the department … _____
e … money at local … _____
f … on. I want to start selling things online soon! _____
g … online for books and clothes, but not for shoes – you can't try them … _____
h … stores. A few years ago I started shopping … _____
i … store, but it's expensive. I prefer to spend my … _____

4 Complete the shopping words.

1 Do you want to g_____ s_____? Let's go now, before the s_____ m_____ closes.
2 At the m_____ you can b_____ meat, fish, fruit, and vegetables.
3 This is a d_____ s_____, so why can't I p_____ b_____ credit card?
4 It's easy to s_____ lots of m_____ with just one click when you shop o_____.
5 She makes clothes and she s_____ them in a few of the l_____ s_____ in her town.
6 If you know your size, sometimes you don't need to t_____ o_____ new clothes.
7 You can only pay w_____ c_____ here. We don't have a credit card machine.

PRONUNCIATION: Sentence stress

5 ▶9.5 <u>Underline</u> the stressed words. Then listen, check, and repeat.

1 He goes swimming twice a week.
2 They watch movies two or three times a month.
3 I finish a book about once a week.
4 We take a vacation in Thailand every year.
5 Do you drive every day?
6 She takes a shower once or twice a day.

Skills 9D

WRITING: Describing a photo

1 Look at the photo and read the e-mail. Find three differences between them.

> Hi Chloe,
>
> How are things? I hope you're well.
>
> I had a great time in London last weekend. I went with four of my friends from college. We took the bus and got there early. First we went to a museum, and then we went shopping.
>
> Here's a photo of us on the street. We're carrying a lot of shopping! There are only three people in the photo because Karol is taking the photo. That's me on the left. Look! I'm wearing the black hat you bought for me. The friend at the top in a T-shirt is David. Paula and Alex are standing next to me.
>
> E-mail me soon, please. I want to know how the concert was.
>
> Izzie

2 Find one mistake in each sentence and write the correct words.

1 There are a window on the right of the photo. _____
2 They are four people in the photo. _____
3 They look in a window. _____
4 David is standing to the top. _____
5 The man in the left is Alex. _____
6 The other woman on the middle is Paula. _____

3 Look at the picture and write sentences.

1 That / our mother / middle
   _____
2 My little sister Sofia / top of the photo
   _____
3 She / sit / on my dad's shoulders
   _____
4 David / middle, next / Mom
   _____
5 There / leaves and grass / bottom
   _____
6 And that's me / right
   _____

4 Choose a photo of you with your family or friends. Write an e-mail to a friend and describe it. Make sure you:
- explain who the people are and their position in the photo.
- use the present continuous to say what they are doing.
- use *there is/are* to say what things are in the photo.

9 REVIEW and PRACTICE

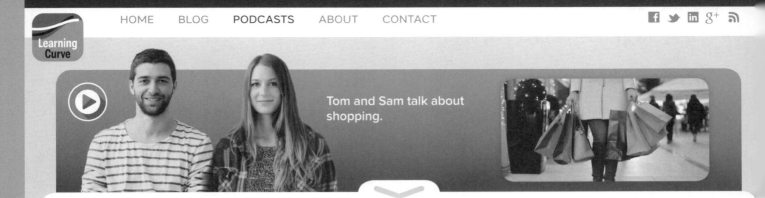

HOME   BLOG   PODCASTS   ABOUT   CONTACT

Tom and Sam talk about shopping.

LISTENING

1 ▶ 9.6 Listen to the podcast about clothes and shopping. Number the clothes 1–10 in the order you hear them.

a boots _____
b coat _____
c dress _____
d hat _____
e jeans _____
f sweater _____
g shirt _____
h shoes _____
i skirt _____
j pants _____

2 ▶ 9.6 Listen to the podcast about clothes and shopping. How often do the speakers go shopping? Complete the sentences.

1 Speaker 1: every _____
2 Speaker 2: _____ times a week
3 Speaker 3: three times a _____
4 Speaker 4: every _____

3 ▶ 9.6 Listen again. Complete the sentences with one or two words.

1 Tom often wears the same _____.
2 Yesterday, Sam and Tom went to Greenway _____.
3 Speaker 1 is buying a _____ and _____.
4 Speaker 1 is paying by _____.
5 Speaker 2 is trying on _____.
6 Speaker 2 always shops _____.
7 Speaker 3 thinks the _____ is horrible.
8 Speaker 3 is meeting her _____.
9 Speaker 4 thinks the _____ has too many colors.
10 Speaker 4 thinks the _____ is beautiful.

READING

1 Read Simon's blog about emojis. Choose the best summary.

a Emojis give people problems.
b Everyone loves emojis because they are quick.
c Simon's friends like emojis.

2 Read the blog again. Choose the correct answers to complete the sentences.

1 Simon's friends _____ send him emojis.
 a sometimes
 b often
 c never

2 He says people _____ a new language with emojis.
 a can learn
 b don't need to learn
 c are speaking

3 He didn't send his sister a message because he was _____.
 a busy
 b surprised
 c angry

4 The message from his friend made him _____.
 a worried
 b bored
 c sad

5 His girlfriend didn't reply because he didn't _____.
 a use the right emoji
 b reply to her message
 c feel excited

6 He doesn't like emojis because _____.
 a they're boring
 b there are too many
 c they can cause problems

REVIEW and PRACTICE 9

HOME **BLOG** PODCASTS ABOUT CONTACT

Guest blogger Simon writes about the little pictures we send on our phones.

Emoji problems

I hate emojis

There – I said it! My friends send me funny pictures every day, but I don't like them. Do you want to know why? OK, but first let's look at why emojis are so popular.

First, they are quick. We live in a fast, busy world, and it only takes a second to send an emoji. Next, they are international. American, Brazilian, Chinese – we can all send and understand messages. And we don't need to learn a new language! And finally, a lot of people think emojis are fun. They make people laugh!

But emojis aren't always good. In fact, they often give me problems. Here are three stories from my life to show you what I mean!

Last year, my sister had an interview for a very good job. She sent me this message: "I got the job!" I was busy and I didn't have time to send her a message. So I sent a "surprised" emoji. She replied with an "angry" emoji. I didn't understand, so I called her later. She asked why I sent her a "surprised" face. "You think I'm not good enough for the job!" she said. But it wasn't true!

An old friend sent me a message with some sad news. I tried to send a "sad" face emoji to him, but I was tired and I didn't have my glasses. And I sent him a "bored" face! The next morning I saw my message and I was really worried! I called my friend and said I was sorry, but everything was OK.

My girlfriend and I went on vacation last year. The night before we flew, she sent me a message. It was a plane, a heart, and a happy face. I tried to reply with an "excited" face, but I did it wrong. I sent her a "scared" face. She didn't reply!

So that is why I don't like emojis. But sometimes I think everyone else loves them! Here are some interesting emoji facts. Did you know ...

- the first emoji was in 1999. A Japanese man called Shigetaka Kurita made it.
- July 17 is World Emoji Day. They chose that date because it is the date you can see on the emoji of a calendar.
- the world sends more than five billion emojis every day.
- the most popular emoji last year was the crying and laughing face. Second was the kissing emoji. And third was the red heart.

UNIT 10 Time out

10A LANGUAGE

GRAMMAR: Present continuous for future plans

1 Order the words to complete the conversation.

A ¹ this weekend / you / doing / what / are?
B ² my grandfather / am / looking after / I. What about you? ³ you / tomorrow / are / studying?
A ⁴ I / am / yes. ⁵ going out / are / on Sunday / you? ⁶ practicing for / we / our concert / are.
B That sounds great!
A ⁷ there / after lunch / is / Patricia / driving. Do you and Tom want to come with us?
B Yes, please. ⁸ in the morning / going / we / swimming / are. You can meet us at the pool!

1 _____?
2 _____.
3 _____?
4 _____.
5 _____?
6 _____.
7 _____.
8 _____.

2 Complete the sentences with the correct pairs of verbs in the present continuous.

> write/finish   do/go   fly/see   help/cook
> meet/take   not sail/drive   run/plan   visit/have

1 I _____ to Brazil on Monday, but I _____ my grandparents there until Friday.
2 We _____ friends tomorrow morning in Rio. We _____ lunch at a restaurant together.
3 _____ you _____ anything tonight? Francine and I _____ to the movies.
4 My sister _____ in the race next month. She _____ to run every day before then!
5 They _____ to Greece tomorrow on their boat. They _____ there, instead.
6 _____ Harry _____ his mother at the airport this evening or _____ she _____ the bus?
7 When _____ he _____ his next book? I _____ this one today.
8 I _____ Izzie buy a new tablet tomorrow, and then she _____ dinner for me.

VOCABULARY: Free-time activities

3 Choose one option in each sentence which is <u>not</u> correct.

1 Are they having a *video / barbecue / good time*?
2 I'm not staying at a *friend's house / tent / hotel*.
3 Please, can we visit *the museum / my parents / a hotel*?
4 Can I watch *a video / the soccer game / museum*?
5 We had the *art gallery / barbecue / party* in our backyard.
6 Let's go to *a festival / a video / the beach*!

4 What are the people going to do? Complete the sentences.

1 I'm ready to relax in front of the TV. I'm w<u>atching</u> <u>a</u> m<u>ovie</u>.
2 Malachi loves history and old objects. He is going downtown. He's v_____ _____ m_____.
3 My parents are seeing their favorite musician. They're g_____ _____ _____ c_____.
4 Paola is tired after work. She wants to take a bath and go to bed early. She's s_____ h_____.
5 He enjoys looking at paintings and photographs. He is v_____ _____ a_____ g_____.
6 We're cooking in the backyard today. We're h_____ _____ b_____.
7 Alice enjoys being outside and seeing her favorite bands. This weekend she's g_____ _____ _____ f_____.

PRONUNCIATION: Sentence stress

5 ▶10.1 Listen and repeat. Underline the stressed words.

1 A Who is she seeing tonight?
   B She's meeting her friends from college.
2 A Are they watching a movie?
   B No, they're not. They're watching soccer.
3 A I'm visiting a friend in Miami.
   B Are you taking the bus?
4 A Is he staying at home this evening?
   B Yes, he is. He's doing housework.
5 A Which beach are you going to?
   B We're talking about that now.
6 A How are we getting there?
   B We're taking the train.

58

SKILLS 10B

READING: Scanning for information

1 Quickly read the guide. Match events 1–7 with A–E. There are two extra events.

1 a movie _____
2 a jazz concert _____
3 a classical concert _____
4 a rock concert _____
5 a festival _____
6 a talk _____
7 an art exhibition _____

2 Underline the key words in each question. Then scan the text for the answers.

1 <u>How many bands</u> are playing on Friday? _____
2 Which event is only in the morning? _____
3 How many events are only free for students? _____
4 How old do you need to be to watch the movie? _____
5 What type of movie is at the movie theater this weekend? _____
6 How much is the art exhibition if you're not a student? _____
7 What time does the event at Cambalache start? _____
8 Which two places are on the same street? _____ _____

3 Complete each sentence with the affirmative or negative imperative of the verbs in the box. There are two extra verbs.

be	book	buy	close	come
go	have	tell	wait	watch

1 _____ a ticket for me at the station. I already have one.
2 Please _____ to the next class with your questions about the movie.
3 I'm working late tonight so _____ for me for dinner.
4 Flights are expensive, so _____ them very early!
5 See you after the party. And _____ a good time!
6 _____ the door. I like it open.
7 I'm putting my coat on now. _____ without me!
8 _____ him I have a present for him. It's a secret.

THIS WEEK'S main events in and around town

A

Battle of the bands FINAL
See the best rock music in town. Three local bands are playing to win the $500 prize – don't miss it!
Friday 16, 8 p.m.
Cellar 21, Cass St.
$12, Students $10

B

Music of the 20s, 30s and 40s
A look back at the jazz of New Orleans. With Charles Rayburn and Lolo Gonzalez and his band.
Cambalache bar, Fenton Street
Saturday 10 p.m. till late!
$15

C

Variplex Movie Theater
Police Force 2 - Action comedy (+12 years)
The second in the Police Force series – the first was exciting and funny!
**** The Daily Show, ****Movietime website
4:30 and 7:30 Sat. and Sun.
Tickets: $8.50 from movie theater box office

D

Talk: "From Dinosaur to Dodo"
Natural Science Museum
Wednesday 10:30–11:30 a.m.
Speakers include Margaret Pearson "TV's dinosaur expert." Come with questions!
Get tickets online before Wednesday for free.
School groups welcome! Find out more at www.NatSciMus.ed.us

E

Fenton gallery
"Down" is an exhibition of landscape paintings and sculptures by local artists. Starts this week for two weeks only.
Monday thru Friday 10–6, Fenton Street, admission $3 (free for students)

4 Order the letters to make words about music and movies. Then write them in the correct category.

| ~~coinat~~ | callsasic | mycoed | adarm | leecorntic | phi-pho |
| rorrho | zjaz | opp | cork | caronem | sceenic oftinic |

types of movie	types of music
action	_____
_____	_____
_____	_____

10C LANGUAGE

GRAMMAR: Question review

1 Order the words to make questions.

1 a museum / did / last visit / when / Fabien
   _____?

2 did / the concert / like / he
   _____?

3 do / go / how often / to / the movies / you
   _____?

4 right now / can / bands / I / see / what
   _____?

5 the festival / was / where
   _____?

6 are / favorite / actors / who / your
   _____?

7 DVD / it / can / on / watch / we
   _____?

8 any / are / making / new movies / now / they
   _____?

2 Match a–f with the questions in exercise 1.

a simple present   _____
b simple present of *be*   _____
c simple past   _____ _____
d simple past of *be*   _____
e present continuous   _____
f with *can*   _____ _____

3 Complete the questions with the verbs in parentheses in the correct tense.

1 _____ you _____ a good book right now? (read)

2 What type of games _____ she _____ playing when she was a child? (like)

3 Who _____ your favorite writer now? (be)

4 How often _____ you usually _____ each year? (fly)

5 How many people _____ at his last party? (be)

6 _____ there lots of grocery stores in your town these days? (be)

7 "_____ he _____ a musical instrument?" "No, he can't." (play)

8 When _____ you _____ shopping with your sister – next Saturday or Sunday? (go)

9 _____ Jean sometimes _____ to jazz? (listen)

10 _____ you _____ that horror movie last night? (see)

VOCABULARY: Sports and games

4 Choose the correct options to complete the sentences.

1 How often do you _____ running on the beach?
   a play   b do   c go

2 I _____ gymnastics when I was a young girl.
   a did   b played   c went

3 I told him I'm no good at chess, but he still wanted to _____ with me.
   a go   b do   c play

4 He _____ yoga on weekends.
   a does   b goes   c plays

5 Last weekend, they _____ rock climbing.
   a played   b went   c did

6 She didn't study much in college. She mostly _____ videogames!
   a did   b played   c went

7 They're _____ soccer in the park.
   a going   b doing   c playing

8 We're _____ skiing soon. I'm so excited!
   a doing   b playing   c going

5 Complete the sports or games words.

1 Does he play h_____ on grass or ice?

2 I did k_____ until I got my blue belt; I didn't get a black one!

3 A b_____ and a t_____ ball are pretty small!

4 Last winter, we went s_____ in the Atlantic Ocean. It was really cold!

5 Most professional b_____ players are more than 6.5 feet tall.

6 I'm doing p_____. It's a bit like yoga.

7 One popular sport people play on the beach is v_____.

8 This weekend, they're going h_____ in the hills while the weather is good.

9 Let's play t_____ tomorrow – with two more people we can play doubles.

10 He couldn't go b_____ yesterday because his bike is broken.

PRONUNCIATION: Intonation in questions

6 ▶ 10.2 Listen and repeat the questions. Pay attention to the intonation.

1 What's your hobby?
2 Are you doing it this weekend?
3 When did you start?
4 Was it difficult?
5 How often do you do it?
6 Is it expensive?

SKILLS 10D

SPEAKING: Asking about a tourist attraction

1 ▶10.3 Listen to the conversation. Number the photos in the order the people talk about these things (1–5).

a ___ b ___ c ___ d ___ e ___

2 ▶10.3 Listen again. Are the sentences true (T) or false (F)?

1 The tourist knows Valparaíso well. ___
2 She and her boyfriend are staying at a hotel. ___
3 She really wants to go to the Pablo Neruda museum. ___
4 The museum doesn't have a gift shop. ___
5 They want to go to the museum today. ___
6 On Saturday, there is an event at the museum. ___
7 They need to pay 2,500 pesos to get in. ___

3 ▶10.3 Read the sentences from the conversation. Which words did you hear in the questions? Listen again and check.

1 Is there a *café / gift shop*?
2 *When / Which days* is it open?
3 What time does it *close / open* today?
4 How do you *get there / pay*?
5 Are there any *concerts / special events* today?
6 What is there to do *if it rains / in the evening*?

4 ▶10.4 Listen to a conversation. Check (✓) the expressions you hear.

1 Did you enjoy your trip? ___
2 How was your trip? ___
3 Did you have fun? ___
4 Oh, OK. ___
5 Oh really? ___
6 Sounds fantastic! ___
7 Sounds wonderful! ___
8 That sounds interesting. ___
9 What's that like? ___
10 Where did you say that you went? ___

10 REVIEW and PRACTICE

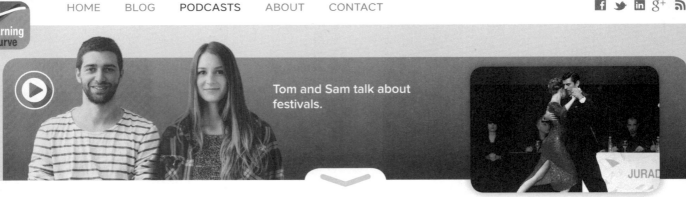

HOME   BLOG   PODCASTS   ABOUT   CONTACT

Tom and Sam talk about festivals.

LISTENING

1 ▶ 10.5 Listen to the podcast about festivals. Complete the table for the five festivals Anna is going to.

	Country	Type of festival
1	China	_____
2	_____	Comedy and _____
3	_____	_____
4	_____	_____
5	_____	_____

2 ▶ 10.5 Listen again. Write T (true), F (false), or NG (not given) if there is no information in the podcast.

1 Sam is going on vacation with college friends for the first time. _____
2 Anna always goes to festivals in the summer. _____
3 The Shanghai film festival only shows Chinese movies. _____
4 Anna is driving to Edinburgh. _____
5 The Edinburgh Fringe festival is a month long. _____
6 Anna's parents live in New York. _____
7 You can't buy anything at the Santa Fe festival. _____
8 Anna is meeting a friend in Santa Fe. _____
9 Anna is dancing in a competition. _____
10 Anna likes Indian music. _____

READING

1 Read Kate's blog about working out. Match the photos with three of the paragraphs (1–6).

2 Read the blog again. Complete gaps 1–6 with questions a–f.

a I can't move very well in the morning. What is the problem?
b My brother says playing videogames can help us get in shape. Is this true?
c Why do people want to exercise? It's so boring!
d You ran a marathon last year. What did you do when you finished? And are you running any more marathons next year?
e I can't sleep at night and I often get sick. What can I do?
f I went running for the first time yesterday. Why are my knees hurting today?

3 Order the letters to make sports and games.

1 e a t r a k   k_____
2 t a b e l l   b_____
3 w i n s g i m m   s_____
4 s h e s c   c_____
5 c o r k   g l i m c n i b   r_____ c_____
6 g i n s i k   s_____
7 n a s t y g i c s m g_____
8 e k b i   d g i n r i   b_____ r_____
9 l a t e b l a b s k b_____
10 k i n h g i   h_____

REVIEW and PRACTICE 10

HOME **BLOG** PODCASTS ABOUT CONTACT

Our guest blogger and "fitness fanatic" Kate answers your questions about getting in shape and staying in shape.

Questions for a "fitness fanatic"

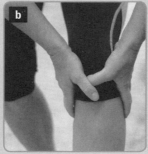

1 _____

I was so hungry after the race. I ate a big plate of rice and a special drink. It's really important to eat a lot after a lot of exercise. But before I ate, I lay down on my back with my legs up in the air – it feels silly but it really helps! As for the future, I'm running the London Marathon next year – wish me luck!

2 _____

I'm sorry to hear that. Were you running on grass or on the sidewalk? Running on hard ground can be really bad for the knees. Try running at the gym. It's less interesting, but it's better for your knees!

3 _____

What type of games is he playing? Because with some games you need to get up and move around. There are dancing games, for example, and games where you pretend you're playing tennis. These games can help you get in shape. But it's much better to actually go dancing or play tennis!

4 _____

I have one word for you – swim! Did you know that swimming every day helps you sleep, makes you happy, and even helps you live longer? And swimmers get sick less than other people. So what are you waiting for? Jump in!

5 _____

Oh, that's too bad! My father had the same problem early in the day. Now he does pilates and yoga every week, and he's like a child again. He jumps out of bed in the morning!

6 _____

There are so many reasons! Some people want to feel good and look good. Other people think exercise is relaxing, and it makes them happy. Do you know the saying "Healthy body, healthy mind"? Exercising can help you think, study, and work. And, of course, it's a great way to meet people!

WRITING PRACTICE

WRITING: Filling out a form

1 ▶ WP1 Listen to the conversation at a bus station. Fill out the 'lost and found' form.

Greyford Bus Services	**Personal details**
Title: Mr. [✓] Mrs. [ ] Ms. [ ]	
First name: *Anthony*	Last name: ¹_____
Street address: ²_____ *Maple Street*	E-mail address: ⁴_____@starmail.com
City, State: ³_____, *Massachusetts*	Phone number: *617-231-3327*
Zip code: *02445*	Date of birth (MM/DD/YYYY): *03/15/* ⁵_____
Details of lost item	
Object: *brown wallet with $40 and credit card*	
Date lost: *02/13/2018 at about 9:30 a.m.*	
Place lost: *bus number* ⁶_____	

2 ▶ WP2 Listen to another conversation and correct five pieces of information.

Greyford Bus Services	**Personal details**
Title: Mr. [ ] Mrs. [✓] Ms. [→]	
First name: *Nithya*	Last name: *Patil*
Street address: *5573 Sycamore Drive*	E-mail address: *nithya@padmail.com*
City, State: *Austin, Texas*	Phone number: *512-527-6906*
Zip code: *79759*	Date of birth (MM/DD/YYYY): *02/01/1989*

3 Write the sentences again with capital letters where you need them.

1 he's in the u.s. but he's japanese.

2 i am from rouen, in france.

3 my zip code is 78759.

4 his sister speaks chinese and french.

5 these are michael's keys.

6 she lives at 6 green street.

4 Complete Michi's form with the information in the box. Use capital letters where you need them.

> 305-555-9846   mrs. fujioka   08/31/1981   miami   40 park street
> 33166   japanese   m_fujioka@starmail.com   michi

Personal details	
Title ¹_____	Zip code ⁶_____
First name ²_____	E-mail address ⁷_____
Last name ³_____	Phone number ⁸_____
Street address ⁴_____	Nationality ⁹_____
Town/City ⁵_____	Date of birth (MM/DD/YYYY) ¹⁰_____

64

WRITING PRACTICE

WRITING: Punctuation

1 Read the blog post about three men's trips to work or school. Match the names with the reasons they travel so far (a–c). Don't look at blanks 1–5.

1 Joshua _____
2 David _____
3 Pat _____

a His family lives far from where he works/studies.
b He doesn't have the money to live near where he works/studies.
c He doesn't want to live near where he works/studies.

Stories of daily commutes*

I'm Joshua. **1**_____ In fact, it takes me over an hour and fifteen minutes to get to work. **2**_____ I do it because the good jobs are in the city, but it's expensive to live there. But why do other people commute long distances?

David Givens has one of the longest commutes in the United States – 600 kilometers a day from the mountains in Mariposa County to San José, California. It's a long trip, three and a half hours each way, but David says it's great because his life in Mariposa is so wonderful, and he prefers it to San José. **3**_____

Pat Skinner leaves home at seven to drive 80 kilometers. **4**_____ But Pat's not an office worker commuting to work; he's an eleven-year-old schoolboy. His mom drives him about 500 kilometers each week so that he can go to a good private school. He does his homework in the car!

How far do you commute each day? **5**_____ Comment below!

*commute – (n and v) trip to work every day

2 Add the punctuation to these sentences. Then match them with blanks 1–5 in the blog in exercise 1.

a at seven in the evening he gets home
b davids house is in the mountains its a clean place far from the cities of the coast
c do you like your trip to work
d every morning, i ride my bike to the station and get on a busy train into the city
e I work in london and, like many people, i spend a lot of my day between home and work

3 Complete the sentences with *and* or *but*.

1 He usually rides his bike, _____ today he's on the bus.
2 Why does Andy walk to work _____ take the train home?
3 Every morning, Breana buys a coffee _____ a cookie at the station.
4 I live _____ work in the same town, so I don't travel far every day.
5 My mother's office is in the city, _____ on Fridays she works at home.
6 They work in the same office _____ go to work together.

4 You are going to write a blog post about a trip you often make (every day/week/month). Use these questions to plan your writing.

- Where do you go?
- How far is the trip (minutes and hours or kilometers)?
- How do you travel?
- Do you enjoy it? Why/Why not?
- Do you travel with other people?
- What do you see on the trip?
- Is the trip expensive/interesting/difficult, etc.?

5 Write your blog post.
- Use correct punctuation and capital letters correctly.
- Use the linkers *and* and *but*.

WRITING PRACTICE

WRITING: Describing yourself

1 Read Olga's personal profile. Then match questions a–f with paragraphs 1–4. There are two extra questions.

- a What are you good at? ____
- b What are your hobbies? ____
- c What's your family like? ____
- d What's your plan in the next five years? ____
- e Where do you live and what's it like? ____
- f Who are you and what do you do? ____

LET'S LEARN A LANGUAGE!

Olga St. Petersburg

1 Hi everyone. I'm Olga from Russia. I'm nineteen. Right now, I'm a student in college. I'm studying teaching, and I plan to teach languages one day.

2 I'm from Yekaterinburg, but I study in St. Petersburg, Russia's second city. I don't have my own apartment – this city is very expensive – but I share a big apartment with four other students. It's near to the college, the park, and a large shopping mall. St. Petersburg is a beautiful city for nine months of the year, but it can get very cold and dark around January!

3 In my spare time, I enjoy reading, listening to music, and learning languages – I speak three already and my Portuguese is OK. Why do I want to improve my English? Because it lets me speak to the world and because I need it if I want to work in a good school.

4 I don't see my family very often because I live so far from home. I have an older brother – he works as a doctor in Yekaterinburg, and he has two lovely children. My younger brother is at school and lives with my parents. My dad is an engineer and my mom is a journalist. She works at home.

2 Read the profile again. Write T (true) or F (false).

1 Olga has a job in a school. ____
2 She doesn't live in her home city. ____
3 Five people live in her apartment. ____
4 St. Petersburg is a lovely place to live all year. ____
5 She only learns languages because she wants to. ____
6 She has two brothers. ____
7 Her mother is a doctor. ____
8 The website is for people who want to learn languages. ____

3 Use the prompts to write sentences with *because*.

1 Abbey / never / go / dancing / very expensive
   _____
2 I / not need / a car / there / stores / near / our house
   _____
3 Jamie / love / weekends / he / sleep / late
   _____!
4 Why / she / do / yoga / ? / want / make friends
   _____
5 I / can / run / today / have / bad knee
   _____
6 Why / I / like / this movie theater / ? / cheap
   _____!

4 Write a personal profile for a language exchange website.
- Use paragraphs.
- Say the language(s) you speak and the language(s) you want to practice.
- Give reasons with *because*.

WRITING PRACTICE

WRITING: Writing informal e-mails

1 Read Sunan's e-mail. Then match sentences a–g with blanks 1–6. There is one extra sentence.

a After that I went to bed.
b Bye for now!
c First, we visited an old castle near Sligo.
d Hi Kristof,
e I hope you're well.
f I wanted to tell you about my vacation in Ireland.
g Then I took the bus to the west of Ireland.

To: Kristof Jansson
Subject: Ireland
Attachment: carla.jpg

1 _____

2 _____ How was your summer?

3 _____ I was excited about taking the ferry to Dublin, but the weather was bad, so I traveled to Ireland two days late. So I arrived late, and I didn't have much time in Ireland. But it was beautiful, and it was sunny when I was there.

First I visited Dublin – it's a fantastic city! ⁴_____ Carla, a friend, lives in a town called Sligo in that part of the country. She was happy for me to stay with her. But when I arrived at the bus station she wasn't there. She thought my visit was the next week, and she was out of town! I stayed at an expensive hotel that night. Sligo is small, and there wasn't much to do, so I went to a restaurant on my own. ⁵_____ How sad! ☹

But the rest of the vacation was great. Carla showed me some beautiful places (see photo).

⁶_____ See you next week.

Sunan

---

2 Complete the phrases with the words in the box.

about   care   hello   how   see   ask   things   well

Starting an e-mail	Asking about the person	Saying why you are writing	Finishing the e-mail
Hi Pete,	²_____ are you?	Did I tell you	⁷_____ you soon,
¹_____ Greta,	How are ³_____?	⁵_____ ...?	Bye for now,
	I hope you're ⁴_____.	I wanted to ⁶_____ you ...	Take ⁸_____.

3 Complete the sentences with the correct sequencers, *after that*, *first* or *then*.

1 Juan was late for the exam. _____, there was a problem with the subway. _____ he missed the train. _____, he got lost when he tried to find the college.

2 _____, I found a recipe for chocolate cake on the Internet. _____ I went to the store to buy the things I needed. _____, I made the cake, but I burned it!

3 Helena and Tara wanted to do something special. _____, they went to the park for a picnic, but it rained. _____ they decided to go to the movie theater, but there were no good movies, so they went home.

4 Carlos was tired after a long day at work. He had a coffee and _____ he went to the station, but he fell asleep on the train. _____, he missed his stop and didn't get home until the next day!

4 Write an e-mail to a friend. Tell him or her about a bad or difficult vacation or trip you went on.

- Start and end your e-mail in a friendly way.
- Ask about the person.
- Say why you are writing.
- Use sequencers to show the order of events.

WRITING PRACTICE

WRITING: Describing a photo

1 Look at the photo and read Tiffany's e-mail. Then choose the correct answers.

1 What did Ollie do last Saturday and Sunday?
 a He played games.
 b He went to a party.
 c He went to a festival.
2 Where was Tiffany at the same time?
 a in college
 b at a concert
 c in the country
3 What were they celebrating?
 a the middle of summer
 b Rut's birthday
 c the end of exams
4 What did they eat at the party?
 a cold food
 b a barbecue
 c nothing
5 How long was the party?
 a It finished at three o'clock.
 b It finished when it got dark.
 c It continued all night.

To: Oliver
Subject: Hello from Sweden!!!

Hi Ollie,
How are you? How was your weekend? Did you have fun at the festival?
I had a great time last weekend. We had a party at Loke and Rut's house in the country because it was the celebrations for the middle of summer. During the day, we had a barbecue, played games, and swam in the lake. You can see lights at the top of the photo – we put them up because the party lasted all night. But it doesn't really get dark – we took this photo at 3:00 a.m!
Rut is the friend on the right. She's sitting in front of Loke. That's me at the top. I'm standing next to Peter. There are two friends playing guitar. They are Phil and Nikolas – they're excellent musicians! The friend on the left is Trudy, from college. And the friend in the middle, sitting next to Phil, is Nils, Trudy's boyfriend. The other two are Rachel and Danilo, friends of Loke. We had such a good time!
See you soon.
Love, Tiffany

2 Look at the photo and match the two parts of the sentences. Then complete a–g with the correct form of the verb *be*.

1 There _____ c
2 Loke _____
3 Phil and Nikolas _____
4 Trudy _____
5 There _____
6 We _____
7 It _____

a _____ great night!
b _____ a friend from college.
c ___is___ a beautiful red building behind us.
d _____ all listening to music in the photo.
e _____ behind Rut.
f _____ playing guitar.
g _____ two people standing up.

3 Look at the photo. Then complete the text with the words in the box.

| ~~in the front~~   left   between   right   in the back |

These are people I work with. The woman ¹ _in the front_ with short hair and gray pants is my boss, Maribel. She's fun! The man on the ² _____ with the short black hair is David. He's the receptionist and he's very friendly. Then the older man on the ³ _____ of the photo is Patrick. He's one of the engineers. Another engineer in my office is Gavin – he's behind Patrick. My best friend is Andrea – she is ⁴ _____ of the photo with a book. And that's me on the left, ⁵ _____ Andrea and David. It's a great team!

4 Choose a photo of a party or celebration. Write an e-mail to a friend and describe the photo.

- Explain who the people are in the photo.
- Use the present continuous to say what they are doing.
- Use *there is/are* to say what things are in the photo.

NOTES

NOTES

NOTES

Richmond

58 St Aldates
Oxford
OX1 1ST
United Kingdom
Printed in Mexico

Corporativo Prográfico S.A de C.V.Calle Dos Núm. 257, Bodega 4,
Col. Granjas San Antonio, C.P. 09070 Del. Iztapalapa, Mexico,
Mexico city in July 2018.

ISBN: 978-84-668-2574-0
CP: 862263
© Richmond / Santillana Global S.L. 2018

Publishing Director: Deborah Tricker
Publisher: Luke Baxter
Editors: Debbie Goldblatt, Laura Miranda, Helen Wendholt
Proofreaders: Shannon Neill, Emma Wilkinson
Design Manager: Lorna Heaslip
Cover Design: Richmond
Design & Layout: Lorna Heaslip, Dave Kuzmicki
Photo Researcher: Magdalena Mayo
Audio production: TEFL Audio

Illustrators:
Simon Clare; Guillaume Gennet and Paul Dickinson c/o Lemonade Illustration Agency

Photos:
Prats i Camps; 123RF; ALAMY/David South, Peter M. Wilson, SuperStock, Felix Lipov, VIEW Pictures Ltd, Hugh Threlfall, Zaid Saadallah, Cultura Creative (RF), Jon Davison, Af8images, Vincent de Vries photography, David Willis, Jenny Matthews, age fotostock, Igor Kovalchuk, ONOKY - Photononstop; GETTY IMAGES SALES SPAIN/cnythzl, David Leahy, NuStock, Thinkstock, kanate, Time & Life Pictures, Grafissimo, zetter, Hero Images, Yapanda, ozgurdonmaz, greg801, Michael Heim / EyeEm, artapornp, Indeed, Csondy, JTB Photo, AzmanL, aomam, FaberrInk, LauriPatterson, Jordan Siemens, Hermsdorf, Innocenti, Icon Sports Wire, Lily Chou, Mike Kemp, Zou Yanju, Baloncici, plherrera, unalozmen, Daebarpapa, Fuse, oatawa, pixelliebe, AndreyPopov, quavondo, mactrunk, Komkrit2101, Yuri_Arcurs, clu, vectorikart, Getty Images, John Freeman, SolStock, ROSLAN RAHMAN, Paul Bradbury, Pingebat, Monty Rakusen, Jupiterimages, Niteenrk, Jodi Jacobson, Gabriel Rossi, Dan Bass, Sascha Kilmer, Siri Stafford, i love images, jarenwicklund, Hulton Deutsch, Jeff Greenberg, Toby Burrows, Tetra Images, Letizia Le Fur, Neustockimages, Richard Levine, StockPhotosArt, Alasdair Turner, Photos.com Plus, Comstock, Veronica Garbutt, Agencia Makro/CON, Claudio Ventrella, LightFieldStudios, DEA PICTURE LIBRARY, Hill Street Studios, Jose Luis Pelaez Inc, Min Geolshik, Johnny Greig, Matteo Lepore / EyeEm, Top Photo Corporation, RubberBall Productions, Wild Horse Photography, Blend Images - Terry Vine, Scott Polar Research Institute, University of Cambridge, smirart; ISTOCKPHOTO Getty Images Sales Spain, shapecharge, kyoshino; TOMTOM; ARCHIVO SANTILLANA

Cover Photo: GETTY IMAGES SALES SPAIN/mixetto

All rights reserved. No part of this book may be reproduced, stored in a retrieval system or transmitted in any form by any means, electronic, mechanical, photocopying, recording or otherwise, without the prior permission in writing of the Publisher.

We would like to thank the following reviewers for their valuable feedback which has made Personal Best possible. We extend our thanks to the many teachers and students not mentioned here.
Brad Bawtinheimer, Manuel Hidalgo, Paulo Dantas, Diana Bermúdez, Laura Gutiérrez, Hardy Griffin, Angi Conti, Christopher Morabito, Hande Kokce, Jorge Lobato, Leonardo Mercato, Mercilinda Ortiz, Wendy López

The Publisher has made every effort to trace the owner of copyright material; however, the Publisher will correct any involuntary omission at the earliest opportunity.